BOOK ENDORSEMENTS

"Tom Wilson gives us research insight and wise counsel for the retirement journey. This book helps us reimagine the next stage of this voyage with the real possibility of growing whole, not old."

—Richard Leider
International bestselling author of *The Power of Purpose, Repacking Your Bags, & Life Reimagined*

"No matter how you feel about earlier stages of your life, Tom's sound advice will help your NEXT STAGE be better. It's not too late to live the life you love!"

--- Rev. Dr. Jim Sherblom
Author of *SPIRITUAL AUDACITY*

"NEXT STAGE comprehensively addresses the dilemma of many successful executives "now what"? Tom Wilson's research and conclusions are a must read for those of us who treasure relevance and meaning independent of age."

--- Thomas F. Casey Jr.
Author of *Executive Transitions 2 Leveraging Past Experience For Future Success!*

Next Stage

In Your Retirement, Create the Life You Want

TOM WILSON

BALBOA.
PRESS

A DIVISION OF HAY HOUSE

Balboa Press books may be ordered through booksellers or by contacting:

Balboa Press
A Division of Hay House
1663 Liberty Drive
Bloomington, IN 47403
www.balboapress.com
1 (877) 407-4847

Because of the dynamic nature of the Internet, any web addresses or links contained in this book may have changed since publication and may no longer be valid. The views expressed in this work are solely those of the author and do not necessarily reflect the views of the publisher, and the publisher hereby disclaims any responsibility for them.

The author of this book does not dispense medical advice or prescribe the use of any technique as a form of treatment for physical, emotional, or medical problems without the advice of a physician, either directly or indirectly. The intent of the author is only to offer information of a general nature to help you in your quest for emotional and spiritual well-being. In the event you use any of the information in this book for yourself, which is your constitutional right, the author and the publisher assume no responsibility for your actions.

Any people depicted in stock imagery provided by Getty Images are models, and such images are being used for illustrative purposes only. Certain stock imagery © Getty Images.

Print information available on the last page.

ISBN: 978-1-9822-2932-0 (sc)
ISBN: 978-1-9822-2934-4 (hc)
ISBN: 978-1-9822-2933-7 (e)

Library of Congress Control Number: 2019907012

Balboa Press rev. date: 08/27/2019

Dedication

"To Martha, Rob and Lauren, John and Ali, and to Sam and to Toby, you all bring meaning and happiness to my life."

To Janet Bruce
You two are the best!
I love your passion + drive,
you are models for us all
Hope you enjoy this book.
all the Best
Tom Huth

Contents

Preface

As you enter the stage of life when you are moving beyond work and raising children into a world that is broad, open, and undefined, you may be finding it both exciting and scary. After all, this is perhaps the first time in your life, and certainly in the lives of millions of people, where there is no one telling you what to do. You can use this time as you wish. The challenge is that you are closer to the end of life than to the beginning. Therefore, you will be making choices, whether conscious or not, about many things in how you live your life going forward. Will you be able to look back on your life and say you did with it what you could and that it was well lived?

This book will explore how to gain insights on where you are, where have you been, and most importantly where are you going. It is a simple concept. If you can understand the road that has been traveled and the nature of what lies ahead, you will be able to make better choices. This book will not provide you with a well-defined, structured view of what to pursue, but it will hopefully provide good questions, resources, and ideas where you can discover and develop your own Master Plan to create the future, the life you want. Then, you can determine how you can realize the greatest value from this gift of time. There are references, tools, rating scales, and concepts to help you develop your personal Master Plan for this next stage of life. You can implement this plan now or when you are ready. You have the ultimate flexibility and authority to decide.

I wrote this book because I was facing many of the questions, challenges, and concerns that you are facing or have faced. The interest grew into a passion, which grew into this book. I have spent my career as a management consultant, and during this time, I've developed a skill of making complex information simple to understand and act upon.

I've written several books in my profession (organizational performance and total reward systems), but I knew I had another one in me. This time, it was not about businesses or organizations—it was about what I was experiencing. So I set about reading, researching, and discussing this subject with friends and colleagues. I interviewed more than thirty people who shared their stories with me and helped me learn what was important to know or do.

I read many books on retirement, and while they each were helpful in one or two areas, they did not give me a full picture of what I was facing. I discovered through this process that several themes kept emerging as driving forces for people in this stage of life. I wanted to provide something that would be helpful to people who are facing big questions in this stage of life. I don't pretend to be an expert in each of these areas, but I can provide information, insights, and guides for helping you make the right decisions. I have done this kind of work all my life.

I want you to read this book thoroughly, but you don't need to follow the sequence of the chapters. I want this book to become a treasured resource for you as you pursue this next life stage. Follow your areas of interest and curiosity, and when you want to know more, there are significant references provided in each chapter and in the resource bibliography that can lead you to further exploration, analysis, and development of your own approach. Use these resources to continue and expand your learning if you want.

I have provided many meaningful resources to help you understand the dynamics, challenges, and developmental tasks of this unique stage of life. There are many short vignettes from the people I interviewed and researched that illustrate feelings, insights, and actions. There is more being developed each year by researchers, thought leaders, and storytellers. I encourage you to continue to follow your interests, curiosity, and heart.

As the old African proverb goes, "It takes a village to raise a child." Well, in writing a book like this, it took a village too. I would like to extend my deep appreciation to the many people who made this book possible. You have each contributed in unique ways to form my thinking, encourage my continued work on this book, and bring information and insights.

First, throughout this book, there are many references to research studies and individuals who have written meaningful works on the various subjects covered in this book. I would like to thank you for your contributions and thoughtful research, and I look forward to learning more about your discoveries and developments as we all seek to address the great questions of living well, living long, and living in harmony.

Second, there are many references to the individuals I interviewed about their stories and experiences. To those who shared your wisdom with me, thank you. Thank you for your time, your openness, and for sharing your ideas, struggles, discoveries, and challenges. Your contributions have enriched this book and given important ideas and inspirations to others.

Third, my wife, Martha, has provided me with continuing encouragement to keep going and space when I needed to dive deep into this manuscript. She has been with me and was a great sounding board for ideas and guidance. She kept me from becoming too superficial or relying on the obvious. She challenged me to go deeper and find what is unique or important about what I was saying. Finally, she was my first editor. She painstakingly read through the manuscript and gave me fabulous feedback and notes. Thank you, honey.

Fourth, thank you to the individuals who provided me with references and guidance as I was developing my own views and ideas. Tom Sadtler, a friend and thought leader on designing what's next in life, gave me helpful information and thoughtful feedback that were very important in the early stages of this book. Doug Hardy—an accomplished author, friend, and extraordinary editorial professional—provided insightful counsel to this book and guided me as I worked to complete the manuscript. His comments and feedback gave me great confidence that this could be a book of importance for many people.

Finally, I want to give thanks to Henry David Thoreau, Ralph Waldo Emerson, and Louisa May Alcott. I spend many hours walking in the woods of Concord (Massachusetts) Town Forest and Walden Woods. I walked the same trails they followed more than 160 years ago. If you are on these trails and listen quietly, you can almost hear their voices. I thought a lot about them while I walked with my dog, Ollie, and while I worked on composing this book. I gained inspiration from these woods, ponds, gentle breezes, and their voices. Thank you, Henry, Waldo, and Louisa May.

I hope this book becomes a treasured resource for you. I know that you will find things that you already know, and I hope you find things that are new. You will find a way to chart your pathway through this important time of life. I hope you try some of the exercises in these pages and go deeper into those areas that spark your interest. There is much to be learned about this life we live and the things you can do to make it one that is well lived. This is an exciting and scary time. Remember, we are facing a different kind of biological clock than when we were young. You don't know when the alarm to pass on will come, and it is your responsibility now to make the most of this next stage.

I am working to do this, and I encourage you to join me. A book has a way of freezing your thoughts at the time when you wrote them down. I know that I will continue learning, evolving my thinking, and discovering new information and insights. If you are so inclined, visit my website and tell all of us your story through the blog posts. Remember that you are not alone; there is much you can offer to others and learn from others. That is one of the most exciting and important dynamics of these times; we are defining what it means to be alive during this next stage.

Now, enjoy and be well,

Tom Wilson

www.MyNextStage.org
Tom@MyNextStage.org

Chapter 1

The Dawn of a New Stage

*Twenty years from now, you will be more disappointed by the
things that you didn't do than by the ones you did do. So,
throw off the bowlines. Sail away from the safe harbor. Catch
the trade winds in your sails. Explore. Dream. Discover.*
—Mark Twain

If you had been born in the early 1900s, your life expectancy would
be no greater than age fifty. If you lived beyond that time, you would
be someone very special. In earlier ages of human culture, warriors
who could no longer hunt for food were given simpler tasks in the tribal
home. Individuals in their forties and fifties were regarded as elders with
wisdom, experience, and skills that were valued by the tribe.

The stage of life that you were in often defined the norms of behavior,
the pattern of expectations for you and your peers. The Hindus offer four
stages of life (ashramas): student (brahmacharya), warrior (grihastha),
householder (vanaprastha) and sage (sannyasa). Erik Erikson, a major
thought leader in understanding stages of life, identified eight stages
of life.[1] Six of these stages focus on the individual from birth to young
adulthood. Then, there are adulthood and old age.

---

[1]   Erik Erikson, *Identity and the Life Cycle* (London: W.W. Norton & Co.,
    1980).

In 1909, the Dutch writer Arnold van Gennep wrote *The Rites of Passage*.[2] This is one of the first Western attempts to publish a description of the stages that people go through in life:

- being born
- coming of age
- marrying
- having children
- joining the circle of elders
- dying

Then, something began happening. Somewhere in the twenty-first century, we've recognized that life is extending to the eighties and nineties and even over one hundred years. There are those who believe that there are individuals alive today who will live to 150 years old.[3] Perhaps there will be a time when people will see this as commonplace. Even if the generation of people currently turning sixty don't live that long, they will still likely have twenty or thirty and possibly forty years of active, useful, productive, and "to be determined" life ahead. It is almost like being twenty-five years old without the need for a career or children. You've already done that. There is a lot more to life than defined by the traditional views of life after working and raising children – retirement.

In this chapter, we will explore the context for understanding life through a series of stages. There is much research about the stages of life, and an increasing amount of research is focusing on this age of retirement. At this point in time, one can look back on one's life and see how it has progressed through different needs, interests, and pursuits. And we are not done with life. We are healthy. We are curious and growing and wanting to make a difference. There are journeys and challenges ahead of us, waiting for us. Within the history of civilizations, this is a unique time. We can appreciate its importance by viewing it within the context of life's multiple stages. The tasks we have ahead are

---

[2] Arnold Van Gennep, *The Rites of Passage* (Chicago: University of Chicago Press, 1961).

[3] "The First Person to Live to 150 Has Already Been Born—Revisited!" *Forbes Magazine*, (February 3, 2013).

different from other times and require a special mastery if we are to make the most of these years.

While Erikson did not focus much on the stages adults experience, he did offer an important lesson for how we grow. Before an individual can successfully move from one stage to the next, he or she develops certain capabilities to overcome the challenges of the current stage and prepare the individual for the next stage. For example, before a child can sleep through the night, he or she must learn to trust that Mom or Dad will be there when care is needed. Learning to trust enables the child to develop to the next stage and ultimately sleep through the night. This skill enables a young child to develop a sense of hope and build trusting relationships. These are the foundational elements of all relationships and of being happy. Before young adults can have relationships and learn what it means to love, they need to experience both isolation and intimacy. From these experiences, they see the complexity of relationships and the value of tenderness, and they discover the meaning of love. This enables them to form committed relationships that may evolve into marriage and children, both centerpieces for experiencing love and enabling the human species to endure.

Conventional wisdom was that when one finished working, then he or she would relax, enjoy leisure time activities, and wait to die. These were to be regarded as the golden years. However, there are approximately ten thousand people per day turning sixty-five, and this will go on for nineteen years or more.[4] These are the baby boomers who are redefining what retirement means and what people do during this time of their lives. They will not go quietly; they never have. This increasingly large group of people wants action, adventure, and meaning in their lives, and many will simply redefine the expectations by their behaviors.

Much has changed, and we are learning about our lives, environments, and bodies. Within developed countries, the average life expectancy is currently over eighty, and some research shows that this expectancy is increasing by three months each year. Medical science has been able to identify and address many illnesses previously thought to be terminal; they are replacing body parts once regarded as physical

---

[4] "Baby Boomers Retire," FACT-TANK, Pew Research, December 29, 2010.

disabilities. This is giving extended life to many people and makes them healthy, vibrant, and active for many years beyond the historically normal life span. This is the first time in the history of humankind when this extended life will be possible for a large number of people. And this is not a temporary change; it is permanent.

One thing is clear: many people have grown throughout life, dealt with many challenges, and created meaningful and admired lives. Those of us reaching retirement age have learned many things so far. As we approach the time when we are no longer needed by our children and our jobs have transitioned to a younger generation, we face the prospect of living another generational lifetime—twenty or more years. We still have our health, energy, curiosity, and passion for adventures. We have become very good at many things, yet we wonder where these skills and talents can be applied. What will guide us as we start and move forward in these years?

Some people can't wait to leave their current employers because they have many things they want to do. They relish the free time and the choices that await them. They have a list of places to travel, people to see, golf or tennis skills to strengthen, and books to read. They worry about some things, but mostly they want to be free and create the active lifestyle they have dreamed about for many years.

On the other hand, there are those who dread leaving their current workplaces. Work provides a meaningful place to be and a feeling of importance. They are challenged, feel the spirit of accomplishment, and have a clear identity of which they are proud. They look at the future as a big, dark hole and wonder what they will do. They also like the income and the benefits that come from working. They know or have heard of others who have died within six months of leaving their jobs. Did they die from boredom or a loss of purpose and meaning? Did they miss an opportunity to pursue freedom? These are people who want to hold on to images of themselves as teachers, specialists, sales professionals, technicians, managers, or executives. They want to get up in the morning and have a place to go and a reason to get the day started and feel the pressure and vibrancies of the workplace. They want to be around young, energetic people; they fear being alone. Yes, they want more time for golf, being with grandchildren, traveling, and engaging in church or social activities. After they have retired, where do they go and what do they do in the afternoon or the next day? Will Tuesday look no different from Saturday?

The father of one of the people I interviewed said about his retirement, "Sometimes I just sit and think, and other times, I just sit." Retirement offers great openings for some and great uncertainty for others. Some look forward to unstructured time, and others fear endless days with nothing meaningful to do. This is a time when one can pursue new, exciting adventures without the constraints of time or commitments, but some people worry about who they are, what they will become, and how to describe who they are to others. For some, the word *retirement* has negative, useless images associated with it. What do you feel when you say, "I'm retired"?

Most of us are somewhere in between. We have ideas about things that we want to do when we have more time but are concerned about the sense of identity and community that we used to have at work. We like the idea of having more than a one- or two-week vacation and being able to find play times during the week when the course or courts are not so crowded. We see some friends having a great time, and we both want to and feel a sense of uncertainty about joining them. It feels like we live in the middle of a paradox. Many questions emerge within us, and we wonder just what to do with this time and whether we'll really be able to make it work. We may have parents who lived a long life or a short life. What does our genetic lifetime clock say about our remaining time? There are more questions than there are answers.

One thing to remember as we face these times of opportunity and concern is that humans are a learning species. We learn, adapt, and develop skills and abilities that often enable us to evolve to the next stage of life. We create the capabilities to build on the skills we have developed. The issues we face now can be addressed by many of the skills and abilities that we currently have. Our challenge is to discover them. The lessons of Erik Erikson apply to us too.

As adults facing this time of great uncertainty, undefined schedules, and unclear identity, we also need to find the answers for how we live. By looking back, we can identify what has given us great pleasure, satisfaction, and meaning. By looking back, we can discover what is unfinished and needs to be redone. By looking forward, we can chart a path to lead us to the next stage of life. Perhaps we can do things that build on our unique skills and abilities—and address those things that were left undone from an earlier age. We can also use this transition to just let go and move on from those things that used to haunt us. This stage is not defined by our obligations to others but by what we want, feel, and can do. This is the *want-to* stage, the go-for-it stage, and the Reinventing stage of life.

This stage usually starts when one is in her or his mid-to-late fifties. The children, if you have them in your care, are for the most part set to leave or have left the household. One may still be working, but the prospects of that next big promotion, that deal that will make you rich, or the goals you have been seeking throughout your career are now behind you. You have done most of what you wanted or could do in your professional life whether in business, professional services, or social services. The career-oriented stage is now behind you, and what is ahead has not yet been defined. It is time to change, reinvent, and reorient your life. And there are always people who are an exception to this direction.

As we come to understand this stage of life, it is important to consider it within a context of life's journey. There are stages we all experienced earlier in our lives, some with great satisfaction and some with guilt and disappointment. Some of these struggles have been overcome, and some remain with us today. We can leave some experiences behind, and others remain and influence who we are. This is not the final stage of life. If we are lucky, there will be stages after this want-to time with different characteristics. We are likely to face times when our world becomes smaller and simpler.

Many people do not fear what happens after they die, but they do fear what happens *before* they die. What kind of condition will we be in, how much pain will we need to endure, and who will be around us at this time? How dependent will we be on others? Will our independence and dignity fall away? Will we live totally dependent on others? We may find that these are the experiences of our next stage or the one after that, but we are not there yet. This is the time for active adults with free time and some level of resources, talents, and interests to live and pursue those things they have dreamed about.

Individuals who are moving into this new era of retirement are facing challenges to develop new structures and activities that create meaning. Individuals at this stage do not have to fulfill the obligations imposed by an employer or family responsibilities, and they need to address a number of important issues to be successful in this stage of life. This is a new stage in the cycle of life, and one can look forward to remaking, reinventing, and rediscovering what is important. Now is the time to create or utilize opportunities that reinvent their lives because life is now much shorter than when they were in their twenties. We are closer to the end of the journey than to the beginning. So, there is a clear sense of urgency.

Attention is now focused on addressing some key questions that will directly impact one's life and one's self-image. What do you want to do now that work obligations and career interests are no longer defining your daily activities? How much income will you need? Who do you want to live with? How do you stay healthy as the challenges to health are harder? Who are you—and how will this identity impact how you live? This is a time for redefining the path, the style, and the nature of your activities.

We are all at some point on the life continuum. Where we have been often defines many of the opportunities and capabilities we have. You may have certain conditions that limit some elements of your life. We all make choices and have constraints in which to live. We may have physical, financial, or relationship restraints on our choices about the future. It is important to understand the true constraints and determine which ones are there because we have chosen to hold on to them. The nature of these restraints differs depending on your age, your amount of resources, and your expectations about what may likely come your way. This includes income and financial investments as well as the cultural, religious, and family habits that define your identity. It may also include certain health conditions that you have to live with or address. We each have a unique package that has defined our lives.

Consider this: This is the only time left where you may be able to make choices about where, how, who and why you want to live your life. You cannot create more time, and you don't really know how much time you have left on this planet. You cannot change the past, but you can create the future. So, if not now, when?

Chapter 2
Ten Stages that Define a Lifetime

You are more than what you have become. You
must take your place in the circle of life.
—Mufasa, *The Lion King*

This book focuses on one particular stage of life where one is no longer raising children or pursuing a career and has an open span of time and life experiences to be realized. We are challenged to reinvent ourselves, our life surroundings, and our activities. One of the major differences from the past is that we are on our own. This will require initiative, energy, and persistence to sustain these changes. Before digging into the unique aspects of this time period, it is important to view this as only one stage in a lifetime. Let's see this stage within the context of a lifetime of stages.

Many of life's situations, choices, and experiences will determine how well we will realize our potential during this stage. If we can understand this time within the context of life stages, then we can realize that this time is part of a cycle of life, has elements of earlier stages, and prepares us for later stages. So, it is important to understand where we are within this cycle. In addition, this may help us both understand and communicate with children or young people who are at a different stage, and parents or older friends who are also at a different stage. We also realize that this particular stage of life is a very important opportunity to address what needs to be resolved and experience those things we've always wanted.

In conducting the research that formed the foundation for this book, I found a great deal of theoretical constructs that describe the human stages of life. The previous chapter highlighted the works of Hindus, Erik Erikson, and Arnold van Gennep. Erikson and others focused on early childhood development. Carl Jung, Sigmund Freud, Carl Rogers, and Robert Kegan described cognitive and emotional development of individuals. Gail Sheehy, Daniel Livingston, and Mary Catherine Bateson published works that describe the emotional and behavior patterns of different stages of adult life. Even William Shakespeare has weighed in with his poem "The Seven Ages of Man." There are many works that describe the physical development of the brain and body, and some discuss the implications on behavior. However, I did not find anyone who offered a simple, balanced description of the entire life span of a person. I was looking for a description of all the stages we go through from birth to childhood to adulthood to death's door.

Consequently, I've developed a framework that hopefully will offer a meaningful description of one's life span. It is based greatly on these previous research studies and frameworks, but it fills in details and descriptions I have experienced and witnessed in others. Hopefully, this will provide greater clarity about where you have been, where you are now, and what lies ahead. This will not likely describe your journey, but there may be elements that provide you with a meaningful perspective and understanding of your experiences. With great respect to these authorities, I offer the following descriptions that—from my experience and research—describe the ten stages that define a lifetime.

Stage 1: Welcome to This World

In the beginning, we are born. Hopefully, the birth creates a healthy baby. The most important influencers in these early stages of life are sensory kinesthetic. We learn from what we can touch, taste, and feel. This defines much of what the early childhood provides as we seek ways to make sense of the immediate world around us. Erik Erikson's work of this stage highlights the importance of developing a sense of trust, autonomy, and fundamental relationships. The needs are simple and basic: food, protection from the elements, nurturing, and comfort.

Meeting these needs helps shape how the brain and other internal elements of the body and mind develop.

The focus of the infant and toddler is on the immediate family. One experiences the connection with one's mother first, then one's father, and then other siblings or others around the home who provide immediate caring and comfort. As we develop a sense of trust and confidence that we will be taken care of, we form the fundamental capacity to feel love, security, and hope. If we live in an environment that gives us what we need, we come to trust the presence of these comforts and form a foundation of love and self-confidence. Then we start to explore and go beyond the immediate needs of the physical self.

This is the time when the individual develops a basic sense of identity and the early stages of what life in this world is all about. Welcome, toddler. This is the time when one moves from being totally dependent on the mother or father for food and protection to creating a sense of one's own identity. They experiment with ways to control and influence the immediate environment to get what is wanted. The foundations for the self are shaped by these early experiences and inherent capabilities and limitations (DNA). It is the time in life where the most learning occurs over the shortest period of time. Anyone who has been a parent and watched a child develop from infancy through being a toddler in two or three short years is amazed at the growth they witness. And this is only the beginning.

Stage 2: Emerging Adolescence

This is the time when the individual moves from responding to the immediate world to exploring what is really "out there." Adolescence usually covers the years from approximately age four or five until ten or twelve years old. The timing is highly dependent on the experiences one has during this period of physical, emotional, intellectual, and social growth. During this period, we often develop our first sense of purpose and accomplishment. We enter a school system and experience and develop relationships with authority figures who are not our parents. We develop relationships with people who are not in our immediate family and create friends who form the first bonds of affiliation outside the family.

The world of the adolescent child expands beyond the immediate family, neighborhood, or primary family circle to include others who may or may not share the same characteristics. We learn to develop friends and create bonds with them. The awareness of the world broadens, and we learn routines and habits that form the foundation for how we experience the world. Do things come easily for the child or must they struggle to get what they want? Can they trust that other people will be there to provide support and provide for their wants and needs? The world still revolves around need fulfillment, but the needs are more complex and sophisticated. The foundations for the individual's expectations and wants for life are being shaped during this period.

Stage 3: Being a Teenager

For many people, this is one of the most challenging periods of life. Like the earlier stages, the physical being grows and matures dramatically. This stage usually begins around the age of twelve and goes till the person is eighteen or twenty. Children experience puberty and the early stages of a physical adulthood. While this is going on, the quest for identity and affirmation by one's peers increases. Abraham Maslow described this stage as the one where self-identity is defined by and is greatly shaped by the group with which one affiliates.[5] The needs for group acceptance are critical at this stage, and the choices made to fulfill this need sometimes create problems or issues that take years to overcome. We face complex pressures to experience intimacy and independence at the same time. This stage of life has multiple sets of conflicts that are often dominated by emotional ties between one's family and peers, changes occurring within one's own body, and relationships with others.

Intellectual capacity and the ability to think for one's self are also major developments during this time period. School, sports, and activities with friends are often the center of one's world, and the development of social groups where one feels a sense of belonging also dominates this

---

[5]   Maslow, Abraham H., *Toward a Psychology of Being*, Sublime Books, 2014.

life stage. Early experimentation with one's sexuality develops during this time period as well. This is driven by a combination of hormonal developments, relationship needs, and peer pressure. We often define our wants, likes, dislikes, and decisions in relationship to our friends; it's all about our friends.

During this stage, we are seeking to find our own voices. The family is still a critical connection for us—even though we often express this by rejection or determination to do the opposite of what our parents want. The strains on the family are often intense, but there are periods of closeness and warmth. It is clearly a confusing time for the family and the individual. We seek to find independence from the primary family but do not want to be abandoned. We test boundaries, challenge authority, and display personal expressions of a potential identity. Like the adolescence stage, these are experiments and may or may not last or have a significant impact on the character development of the child.

Stage 4: Exploring Adulthood

This stage starts to emerge when the individual reaches eighteen to twenty years and goes till one is in their late twenties. The development of Western societies has in large measure created this stage. Historically, this was a time when the individual would enter the workforce, become married, and assume their position in society, but in most developed nations, this is the time when the individual leaves their primary home for either college or work or both. While they may not physically move out of the home, their orientation to life is no longer based on the home. The individual at this stage is learning what independence truly means. They are narrowing the range of choices or experimenting with lifestyle choices in a deeper and more sustained level. It is still a time of major growth and development, of experiences and learning to live on one's own. This is a time when the person truly does develop a sense of self.

This is a time when we start to understand what consequences mean. There is scientific evidence that the brain is developing a frontal lobe, and the executive function capacity grows to maturity during this stage. While a teenager cannot often understand the impact of their actions (often creating frustration by the parents), individuals at this time start to develop physical capabilities and truly understand consequences. We start to give our parents a little more respect and can anticipate the impact of our actions. We start to experience regret, guilt, and shame more deeply than when we were teenagers.

This is a time of transition and finding direction. Many of us expand our education through college or perhaps graduate school. We may take a job that is appealing or is something our peers have enjoyed. While the jobs may not last for long, they provide experiences that help us understand our likes and dislikes about the employer and the type of work we want to ultimately do. We may pursue adventurous activities for long periods—backpacking and hiking for weeks or months at a time or skiing, surfing, or traveling abroad. There are experiences with friends as well, and we may form a core circle of friends or find a level of independence that was sought at an earlier stage. This is still a time of exploration and growth and trying things out to see if they provide meaning and purpose.

The exploring adult forms deeper relationships now. These relationships may be with the opposite gender or the same one. A primary relationship may develop here, and it may seem primary at least for a while. Some will get married, and others will do a trial by living together. Commitment is not yet a major force in life, but it is testing to see and learn what we like, dislike, and want from a relationship. We know that at some point in the near future, things are going to change. Commitments will be necessary, but we are not ready to make commitments yet.

Similar to the adolescence, the young adult at this stage seeks to find his or her own voice. We are less influenced by what others think and more influenced by what we want and believe. We become engaged in the broader world to make a real and positive difference. We are idealistic and restless. This is an exciting time of life. There are little or no responsibilities except to ourselves. There can be a wonderful sense of opportunity and a sense of freedom that did not exist at earlier stages in life.

There is often hope and belief that we can truly impact the world, and one's passion and voice need to be heard. Joining groups, gangs, organizations, and social networks all promote broader platforms for creating a world with our desired vision. This world could be in our profession, community, neighborhood, town, country, or broader world. This is a time when we can take on these initiatives, and as Bob Dylan once said in a song, "Get out of the road if you can't lend a hand, for the times they are a-changing." Ultimately, with these experiences, conclusions, and questions in hand, we evolve to the next stage.

Stage 5: Realizing Adulthood

The realizing adult starts to take shape in the late twenties and lasts until the late thirties. It is a time when we start to address the decisions that will define the course of our lives. The pathways of what we like and don't like to become clearer from the previous stage, and they become real and important. There is a sense of urgency to make decisions, but we are still uncertain about what to do, where do to it, and who to do it with.

In the exploring adulthood stage, the individual is still experimenting—trying to figure out what they liked doing and who they liked doing it with—without the control of the primary family, but at this stage, we need to make our decisions. The influencers of behavior shift from the family to the self. The time for making commitments is upon us. This is a scary time that has a real sense of urgency, a feeling of loss of our youth (we pass age thirty during this stage), and serious concerns about making mistakes in our commitment choices. You realize this is the time to make these decisions.

This shift is experienced when we start to think about how we can make an activity or area of interest something we will make a living at and make it become (at least for the foreseeable future) our life's work. We can decide to go back to school to get a specialized degree in business, psychology, engineering, marketing, or medicine. We have been on our own in the world for a few years and have learned some of the things that provide a sense of responsibility, meaning and interest, and perhaps passion, but now is the time to make some important commitments.

In addition to the professional life, there is a desire to form a more enduring relationship. For many, this is a time when people get married.

This is perhaps ten years later than in earlier generations. Marriage is fundamentally a statement of commitment to another person. While the intent is to have this relationship last for the remainder of one's life, there is ample evidence that many of these relationships will end in divorce. The commitment may be verbally and truly intended to last forever, but in reality, it will be for as long as the relationship is honest, loving, and meaningful.

Our interest in having children starts to become more important. While there is still a belief that there is sufficient time, for many women (and men), the awareness that there is a biological clock becomes present. They realize that waiting much longer may make it more challenging to have a healthy child. There are significant advances in medicine, but there is an emerging deadline. We also may calculate how old we will be when our prospective children enter college.

So, this is a stage where we make a lot of critical decisions and commitments. What to do with our lives, how to make a desired living, where to live, and who to live with are fundamental questions that are shaped by the experiences of the previous stages and wants for the subsequent stages. We will see later that many of these questions are the same one faces during the Reinventing Adulthood stage. However, for people in this stage, the future is viewed as unlimited. While there may be challenges, disappointments, and great joys, the life span of time is usually not relevant. The important outcomes emerging from this stage are the commitments that will define our futures—at least for the foreseeable future.

Stage 6: Professional Adulthood

This stage of life sees some of the greatest advances in lifestyle, income, and building a family. The primary experience at this stage of life is building a foundation for the family, home, and career. We start seriously settling down and becoming a parent or defining a relationship without children. We advance in our careers, deepen our competencies, and seek to become successful at our chosen professions. The general time span is from the late-thirties to approximately fifty years old. There are many things going on at this stage, but most of them are external to the individual: work, career, family, relationships, friends, where we live, money, sports, and how we live.

From a career perspective, this is the time when we expand our knowledge, skills, and competencies in both depth and breadth. We become true professionals in the fields we have chosen, including child-rearing, and many will advance into roles of management or technical or community leadership. Several significant promotions are usually experienced if we are successful in acquiring and demonstrating our competence.

Like it or not, we become established in the field or expertise areas we have fallen into or pursued from earlier stages. This is the time when we make the most direct impact on our areas of focus or employers, and we may see the greatest growth in personal income. We move from being the "new kid" to being the "master of the ship." We move from looking up to others to being the one others look up to. If we are successful, this is the time when the most progress is realized, and it may be the time when a major career change is made. We may sail through a midlife crisis or redefine and reinvent ourselves into something that is closer to what we truly want.

From a home-base perspective, one of the major areas for development is building a family and defining a role within the family. Men and women at this stage are usually married and start having or adopting children. They create a family unit that builds experiences around the family unit. This means setting up family rituals, taking family vacations, buying a house or condominium, connecting with a community, finding a religious or social community, and setting down roots. While the relationship with the parents is always present, it seems that they are more interested in building relationships with the grandchildren. This creates a sense of continuity of the family tree and builds new traditions, expressions, legacy, and family norms. We seek to raise our children better than our parents did for us.

At this stage, we start to see some limitations of the body that come from aging. The body just doesn't seem to recover from the strenuous activities as quickly as it used to, and flexibility has decreased. In some cases, the individual is witnessing the aging of his or her parents. Women are having greater difficulty having children, especially those who waited until their early forties to do so. They see the impact of their biological clock decisions on both their ability to have children, their interest in sex, and stamina for excessive exercise. Many will significantly increase their exercise routines with the hope that they will regain their stamina, strength, and postpone the aging process. They may investigate numerous health-promoting vitamins, medications, and physical routines (i.e. yoga) that strengthen the body, mind, and spirit. This behavior is more important now because the individual starts to realize the limitations and changes to their physical being.

As we approach the age of fifty, we start to see the world and ourselves from a different perspective. We often start to see life in stages. We see where we have come and how we have changed. We see the lives of our parents or other elders with whom we have relationships. If we have children, we see how quickly they develop through the stages that were described earlier. The end game is still not in view, but at this stage, we start to understand the arc of life and some of the changes that may lie ahead.

For now, we have a lot of responsibilities with work, family, relationships, community, and friendships. We have to get the kids to soccer practice, piano lessons, gymnastics, and youth group meetings. Did I mention dinner and helping them prepare for that big test? Thinking about the future will just have to wait until the never-ending to-do list is completed.

Stage 7: Pinnacle Adulthood

If we survive the previous stages of adulthood, this is the time when we really are at the top of our games. We may have reached the highest points we're going to reach in our careers. We may consider this the prime of our lives. We have become the best at what we do. We may be the leader of some company, organization, or professional team. We may be successful at raising great children who are off to pursue their own lives. We may have become established members of our communities, churches, or social organizations, and we may have reached a pinnacle of life. The age range for this stage is from about age fifty to midsixties. It is time for great satisfaction at what we have accomplished.

By this time, we have celebrated our fiftieth birthdays and realized that more than half of our lives are over. We have done what we can do, and we are either satisfied with what we have accomplished or disappointed in where we are. In most cases, we may feel a little of both. It is a time where we examine what has been done and realize that we have only a few more years to do what is left undone. It is a serious time of life, and there may be serious concerns about the state of one's life and present conditions. We may feel the need to take action professionally or personally to accomplish critical life goals.

The family unit is changing as well. The children at this stage are starting their own life journeys. They no longer view the family as the primary focus of their existence. We have to find some level of peace and satisfaction with this change in the perspective of the children. There will be feelings of relief, satisfaction, and sadness. The family unit may become an empty nest during this stage, and the noise, confusion, excitement, transportation tasks, tension, pressures, and commotion of the children and their friends are gone. The house is quiet. There is room in the refrigerator, and the dinners are simple.

The cost of paying for college or advanced education is putting additional pressure on the family budget and living arrangements. We start to really worry about whether we will have enough money to retire because the stage of retirement is coming closer. Consequently, we usually do not feel free to go and enjoy whatever we want, but we know the importance of these financial worries. How can we build a retirement nest egg and still pay for college or help with the children's living expenses? And what about our parents and the changes they are undergoing? Financial pressures come from all sides: meeting daily living expenses, saving for or paying for college educations, saving for retirement, and replacing that aging car or washing machine.

The body is another area of concern and possible worry. Stamina isn't what it used to be and is even less than in the previous stage. The flexibility and ability to stretch, hit, run, and reach are just not what we once had. Accepting this is important—and so is continuing to strengthen ourselves, stretching, and retaining our strength. We may know someone who has fallen to a major disease. A friend or family member may have died from an illness or be facing serious physical limitations. Health starts to come into periodic discussions, but these are usually short-lived conversations, and we don't want to share too much private information. After all, this is the time in our lives where we are supposed to be at the top of our games.

It is a time to complete the mission or goals we have set out for ourselves earlier in our career. It is a time to accept that we probably won't be able to get that next job, promotion, recognition, financial windfall, or nest egg we have been striving for. We have reached the pinnacle in our careers and need to plan for what is next. Our futures are no longer based on advancing our careers. It is a hard time for achievement-oriented people. However, if we look around at what has been accomplished, this is a time to feel that the job has been done well. It is also time to start thinking about what comes next.

Stage 8: Reinventing Adulthood

This stage is the primary focus of this book. It is unique because we have moved on from our jobs, careers, raising children, and now face (hopefully) twenty to thirty years of "to be determined" life in front of us. We are still generally healthy, curious, and interested in many things, regretful for what we have not accomplished, and worried about whether we will become bored and old.

Some individuals approach this time with great excitement and adventure. We are free to pursue activities and interests that we have been suppressing for most of our working lives. This means travel, time with grandchildren, engagement in social justice initiatives, involvement in church or social organizations, reading books, taking classes, going to the movies in the middle of the week, or spending time with friends. Other people fear the loss of daily challenges, exchanges with coworkers, staying current, feeling a sense of purpose and contribution, and a steady income. We worry that we will become bored and will lose the structure of getting up each day with someplace to go. Most of us are feeling a bit of both.

As we enter this stage, whether it is gradually over a period of years or dramatically (leaving work on Friday and staying home on Monday morning), we initially commit ourselves to doing those things we always wanted to do. We become very active and often fill our calendars with many things. We may become busier than when we were working. After a period of time, we lose some interest in these activities and start to worry that we are falling back. There may be additional worries about our health or our financial conditions. The relationships we've had for years may be strained by our being home every day. Then, we become accustomed to our free time and lack of structure and seek to be engaged in those things that really matter. We are in many ways reinventing our lives and the way we are. We realize that time is not on our side and that this really is the time to do some things differently.

There are two important realizations that emerge during this time. First, we start to accept those things we cannot change about our lives and let go of those things that used to worry or drive us crazy. Second, we need to address some core questions that are starting to loom large in our consciousness. These questions are very similar to those when we were in our thirties, and we need to make more decisions and commitments. Now, the context is different. Our time horizon is not unlimited; it is limited. We feel a sense of urgency, discomfort, and nervousness—as well as excitement, freedom, and eagerness. These mood swings are common and experienced by many.

From a historical perspective, this is a new stage in the cycle of life. We are writing the norms and guidelines for future generations. Our challenge is to discover and create the life we want. This is likely the first time you can do this without the expectations or pressures of creating a career or raising a family. It is your time to use it as you wish. For the next stage, things will be different.

Stage 9: Consolidating Adulthood

In this stage, we are no longer able to move around as freely as before and may have serious limitations. While we may still be able to do certain things we love doing, the range is more limited. This is a time that may occur in the midseventies to late eighties, depending on how well we have kept ourselves healthy and in shape, and our genetic patterns of health. We carry on in this stage till the final stage of life—in one's late eighties to past one hundred. It is a time to let go of the wants that were not accomplished and embrace the things we cherish. Time is less focused on the future and more focused on the present and the past. Activities are defined more by what we can do and still want to do.

Science and technology have made significant advances in the ability to extend the quality of life. During this stage, we may still be very much alive, active, and mentally alert. We become frustrated by the lack of physical abilities while our minds at times still want to do those things we did earlier. At the same time, immense pleasure is derived from simple things like conversations with children, grandchildren, great-grandchildren, friends, and companions. Pleasure is realized from doing games, eating good meals, drinking good wine, attending lectures or shows, and going on limited adventures. This is the time, more than ever before, where we are here and now.

Consolidating means that we are taking this time to get rid of things we no longer want or need and are simplifying our lives. Consider the elderly parent that is giving away the family treasures to her kids; she is sending to Goodwill or recycling centers the old furniture, clothing, books, dishes, and tons of stuff that were collected through one's life. "What do I do with all the silver and china that my mother wants to give me?" is a common refrain from children. A lot of this will just need to be discarded or recycled. It is no longer wanted or needed by the children, and it has only symbolic or legacy value to the individual.

For some, this is a cleansing experience, and for others, this is very hard and sad. It is a recognition that the stuff we collected through our life adventures and achievements is no longer valued. This is often very hard to accept. It is like saying goodbye to old friends or things that gave us comfort and pleasure in the past. The important task is to do this now so that it is not a burden placed on the children. You really don't want to leave attics, basements, closets, and garages full of stuff that the children will need to contend with. Do you?

The world is smaller for us in this stage of life, but it is still meaningful, and the forces of life are strong. An important element of this stage is the community we have developed over time and the richness that comes from these family and friendship connections. We may need to give up the car keys (or have them taken away by children or the police) and learn new ways to retain our independence.

There is significant research showing that the health one experiences at this stage has more to do with love and relationships than with medical treatments. There is little interest in generating income, but we still want to feel that we are somehow making a contribution to the larger world. The "world" could be a country club, social club, church, political or social cause, extended family, assisted-living community, or neighborhood. The importance of these relationships is to assure us that we are not alone for the next stage, and we become ready for the final stage of life.

Stage 10: The Final Stage—Transcendence

At this stage, the end is within sight, but the time, place, and cause may not be known. The end remains uncertain. For many of us at this stage, what is on the other side is not scary, but the process of getting there is. We worry about the pain that we may endure and not being capable of doing basic functions. We fear the loss in our sense of dignity and being alone.

We may feel sad that we won't likely see our grandchildren graduate or get married.

The transformation that occurs when we have fully accepted the limitations and the present condition is remarkable. We have addressed the issues of our sense of accomplishments and integrity and let go of the sense of despair and loss. We are witnessing the death of many of our friends and family members. We require assistance with some of the basic elements of living, and we mistrust our own capabilities (walking, standing, climbing steps, bathing, etc.).

We have probably given up our ability to get around on our own. We now depend on others to push or walk with us to get to places— even to the dining room or bathroom. It is no wonder we experience dependence, sadness, loss, and frustration. We may be ready to die and are tired of waiting. The pain and lack of hope for the future weighs heavy, and we wish there was some easy way for us to end this life. We are ready. We may want to end our lives on our own terms: with family around and without having to endure endless hospital treatments. We have done all we wanted to do, and now all we face is days with pain and simple challenges. Living with continual paid is hard, but we can still enjoy times with family and friends. We are still very much alive and want to be treated with respect and as adults (at least for most of the day).

At the same time, there can be a level of peace and acceptance, and of love and friendship that can transcend these pressures. We have reconnected with our children and rediscovered or expressed the love that should have been part of our earlier stages of life. We at times also experience a deep and powerful sense of transcendence.

It is often difficult for family members to understand, accept, and empathize with this person who used to be so vibrant but now is so dependent on others. They see the complexity, frustration, and limitations. They know that they may be in the same situation someday: waiting, waiting, waiting for death to come and bring peace. We may be angry and resentful and lash out at the ones we love. We may feel sad, ashamed, or incapable of doing the things that used to be so natural and easy. And we may feel a peace that is deeper than ever experienced in life's earlier stages. On any given day, we may experience all of these and more. We are getting ready to let go and realize how wonderful the life we really have had.

This is not a pleasant time of life, but it has a quality of transcendence that can be remarkable. Erik Erikson refers to this stage as *gerotranscendence*. This is a time when there is a shift in the mind-set from the materialistic and logical to more cosmic, transcendent, and spiritual, which can be followed by an increase in life satisfaction. This satisfaction is deeper and more profound than one ever has experienced in an earlier stage of life. It is a deep satisfaction that one has truly had a wonderful life, and for whatever happens next, this life was worth living.

Stages Define a Lifetime

Our life cycle is a circle, or perhaps it is a spiral. It starts, grows, changes directions, circles back to a different spot, and ends. Many of the characteristics we started with as infants, we experience again in the final stage. In the final stage, the ones taking care of us are not our parents; they are our children or professional caregivers. These are people who truly give us care. The journey through these stages has taken us through many challenges, experiences, times of intense pleasure and intense pain, and everything in between. Seeing life in stages gives us a perspective on where we have been, where we are, and what lies ahead. Each person's story and experiences are different. That is the beauty of life's poetry.

Ultimately, we are responsible for who we are, what we did with our talents and tasks, and how we feel about these experiences. We ultimately must play the cards we were dealt, but how we play the hand will define how we will feel about the game. The life you lead speaks for you. It is who you are and what you have become. We cannot change the past; we can change the future. What an amazing journey this is.

As Erik Erikson tells us, each stage provides its own experiences, and these prepare us to meet the challenges of the next one. Regardless of which stage you are in, deepen the enrichment of this experience and know that if you are lucky and resourceful, you will progress ready for the next stage. You can now see where you came from, where you are, and where you are going. You can use these insights to gain the most from this stage and this life.

Chapter 3
Reinventing Adulthood ·

What makes you grow old is replacing hope with regret.
—"Too Many Memories,"
Sung by **Tom Rush,**
Written by **Stephen Bruton**

Today's retirement has many faces. Stephanie sold her consulting business and promptly headed off to Asia. She had always wanted to travel and experience life in these countries, and she spent several months deepening her experience in these cultures. Paul has stepped down from the chief executive officer position at a mid-tier insurance company and wants to do more than just play golf. He is serving on a few boards of directors for nonprofit and small growing companies. He shares his experiences and helps them address their challenges. Mark was a superintendent of a school system, and while his golf game has improved immeasurably, he is working with a colleague to develop leadership workshops for emerging leaders in educational systems, and he is working on immigration issues in his part-time home in Arizona. Ann's business partner recently died, and she is transferring the leadership of her firm to the next generation so that she and her husband can travel. They realized how uncertain life truly is. Harold is retiring from his company as a highly experienced machine operator with some retirement savings but no pension. He wants to continue to earn income to support him and his wife, but he doesn't want to work as much as he did before. He said, "These old bones aren't what they used to be." Lori is now on to her third career with the same energy

and excitement as she had in previous ventures. The focus this time
is to support a nonprofit organization where she can help support the
fulfillment of their mission. Dick is a retired physician and continues to
work between two and five days per month, but he mostly likes to plan
and take adventure biking trips with his girlfriend, Kathy.

This is today's retirement generation. Each of these individuals is
heathy and pursuing passions and interests. They are pursuing exciting
opportunities and enjoying the flexibility from their previous work
schedules. Mary Catherine Bateson refers to this time as the "Second
Adulthood."[6] Gail Sheehy refers to this time as "Adulthood II."[7] Jane
Fonda refers to this stage in her life as the "Second Act."[8] It is clear
that this time is unique in the history of humankind. It is not that the
additional twenty plus years of a life span have been spread across all
stages of life; they have been primarily added to this time when people
no longer have work or family obligations and can make free choices
about what they do. There are many other terms applied to this time
of life, but it is clear that the old associations of retirement as a time for
leisure and entertainment no longer apply to today's generation. This is
why I call this next stage of life "Reinventing Adulthood."

This is the first time in human history when so many people have
been so healthy beyond the years of raising children or pursuing their
professional careers. If you are in this stage, you have the prospect of
living twenty to thirty or possibly more years of active, healthy, engaging
time with no obligations other than doing what you want. This is the
time in life when you are no longer looking for career advancement or
complying with the obligations of an organization—unless you want to.
The structure that once defined daily routines now needs to be replaced
by activities and initiatives that you create to provide meaning and
purpose to life. This is a time when you need to assess where you are
financially, physically, and emotionally and chart a new course for your
life if needed. For many people, this is a scary time, and for others, it is
a time of immense excitement and freedom. For most of us, it is both.

[6]   *Composing a Further Life: The Age of Active Wisdom*, Vintage Publisher, 2010.
[7]   *Passages*, Ballantine Books, New York, 1995 and *New Passages*, Ballantine Books, New York, renewed 2004.
[8]   *My Life So Far*, Random House, New York, 2005.

This is the life stage where the individual is truly in charge to identify, create, structure, pursue, and fulfill what they want. For many, this feels like the Realizing Adulthood stage of life. In fact, there are many common dimensions.

In *The 100-Year Life*, Lynda Gratton and Andrew Scott describe the unique nature of this time from a historical perspective:

> One thing is clear—there will be many pioneers. Neither individuals, nor communities, nor corporations or governments have worked out how best to support a 100-year life span. There are few role models, as even those who live to 100 rarely expected it. We now need to plan with the expectation of a long life. The younger you are, the more you are likely to experiment and the greater the opportunity you have to start and plan afresh.[9]

This is changing the conception we have about post-work and family years and creating opportunities for individuals to redefine themselves in new ways—with new careers or pursuits of interest.

Erik Erikson says the central issue of people at this age is to resolve integrity versus despair. He defines integrity as the thinking process where you examine life and all the choices and experiences you have had and determine whether your life is viewed as integrated, fulfilling, and whole. If not, Erikson says, the feeling will be one of despair and disappointment. Despair is that feeling where the individual sees his or her life as not having turned out as they would have liked—and it is too late to do anything about it.[10] Sheehy says, "It is based on a spiritual imperative: The wish to integrate the disparate aspects of ourselves, the hunger for wholeness, the need to know the truth."[11] For most of

---

[9]   Gratton, Lynda and Andrew Scott, *The-100 Year Life: Living and Working in an Age of Longevity*, Bloomsbury Business Publications, New York, 2017.

[10] Erikson, E. H. (1980). Identity and the Life Cycle. London: W. W. Norton & Co.

[11] Sheehy, Gail, *New Passages: Mapping Your Life Across Time*, Ballantine Books, New York, 1995.

us, this will be a time where we feel satisfaction about what we have accomplished and let go of the disappointment for what was not.

The challenge you face at this stage is utilizing the next period of life to create experiences that are consistent with your capabilities, values, vision, and needs for your life. For some, this will be repairing holes perceived in one's life. For others, it will be doing things they always wanted to do but haven't had the time. For most, it is both. Some of us face real limitations in this period of life due to the health of spouses, children, parents, or selves. The challenge will be to understand what you want to do and can do in light of these responsibilities. How these are resolved will define the course of one's life in this most special and unique time.

Transitioning into a New Stage of Life

Moving into this next stage often starts gradually. There comes a time when you start considering what you are going to do when you leave your current employer or chosen profession. The word *retirement* comes into your awareness. This thinking starts small, and then it becomes more prevalent and important. You start thinking about this and feeling increasingly intense emotions. You have not made any decisions yet or changed anything external about your life, but something has changed in the way you look at what you are doing on a day-to-day basis.

You may discuss this with your spouse, significant other, partner, or close friend. Questions and ideas slowly seep into your consciousness, and you think about this more and more. You're feeling a sense of excitement and fear, of passion and regret, of curiosity and denial. Questions emerge, and you start making lists or doing some reading about what others do. It may feel like something is cooking on the back burner all the time.

John K., who recently turned sixty, said that he has started thinking more and more about what comes next. He loves his work as an attorney but is tiring of the routine. The work doesn't quite have the same challenge and stimulation it once had. He has a number of friends who have reached their mid-to-late-sixties and are winding down their professional careers. His wife is very active and engaged in several dynamic nonprofit organizations. John wonders when he will make this change and—more important—how. Like John, you may be thinking about what this means, what you will do with your time, and what seems like a thousand more questions.

The traditional image of retirement is that period in your life when you *should* relax, play golf or another leisure sport, and do whatever. You are not expected to contribute to society because you have already done that. You should be satisfied with just improving your golf score, having dinner with friends, traveling to tourist sites of the world, and taking naps. You deserve this time of rest and relaxation. This is what *retirement* means historically to many people. What does this word mean to you?

Leaving the structure of an organization or a working career where you have invested a great deal of your life is unsettling. You became dependent on work's demands to define your daily activities and identity, but now, the obligations are gone. The day may be forced upon you, or you may have the ability to gradually transition to this new place over several years. You have moved from a workplace environment that defined your identity to a time that is new and undiscovered. This is now a time when you don't need to rise so early, face the morning rush hour traffic, or miss dinner because of an important meeting. The days now are freer and less structured. This is both scary: "What am I going to do with myself when everyone else is going off to work"—and liberating: "I can do what I want and when I want to do it."

This uncharted sense of transition may last a few weeks or months. Active people often become restless and impatient and want to get into things that are of important value. They have done this all their adult lives. Lori saw this time in her life as terrorizing and exhilarating. She enjoys the challenge of most everything new that she does. She dives into these ventures deeply, gives them a "100 percent plus," and frequently has been very successful. She did this in architecture, in fashion design, in sports, and now in her work with nonprofit organizations. Her mother always said she could do whatever she wanted, and she has worked to realize this promise. So, when it came time to transition to this next stage, she found the lack of structure scary and the freedom to define what and when she wanted as exciting. Like the artist she is, she saw her life as a blank canvas where she can create something new, meaningful, and unique. She was ready to take on this responsibility.

A complicating factor in this transition period is the changes needed by the spouse. He or she needs to make room for the reinventing person, and this presents some obvious challenges. Accommodations also need to be made with expectations about changes in home responsibilities by both examining how things will be different and determining how to adjust things that will strengthen the new living arrangement. Will you create or expand your home office? In addition, the relationships with people you used to work with and connect with will change. The daily check-in conversations have stopped. There is not much happening in your new world unless you create it.

In the interviews and research that formed the foundation of this book, a consistent set of questions that kept emerging. The questions were simple, and they were deep and profound. Each person had a slightly different view of the challenges they were facing. Some questions were irrelevant, and some questions were core issues. These questions may appear to be specific, but they are all highly interrelated.

The primary questions that people in the Reinventing Adulthood stage are thinking about are discussed below. The chapters that follow go into each of these questions in more depth and offer some helpful tools to address them. In my experience, the answers to these questions provide the information one needs to develop an important and meaningful Master Plan. This plan, and the implementation of this plan, can help you create the life you want. This is the best time in your life when you can take command and define how you will utilize this gift that has been provided for you: time.

1. What do want to you do with your time?

This Reinventing Adulthood stage of life has one overarching challenge that was not as significant in earlier stages of life. What do you want to do with your time? This is not simply about how you spend the hours of each day. It's about what you can and will do to bring meaning, a sense of purpose, and fundamental satisfaction to yourself. You are no longer obligated to meet someone else's schedule. You may need to earn income or be limited by certain life conditions. This is the time for you to examine how you can use your talents, experience, energy, and interests to shape who you are during this next stage.

While the challenge of addressing this question may sound daunting, the process of reflecting on those times when you were most enriched by the experience and looking around at what has been left undone may provide you with a pathway. This will help you discover a sense of purpose. Much has been written about purpose and the value it provides to the individual. We will examine these findings. If a purpose does not help you make decisions, it is not your purpose. At this time in your life, you make choices about how you spend your time, talents, and energy. Research has shown that people live longer when there is a sense of purpose, meaning, and engagement in the things one does. And meaning is more important than happiness. Happiness comes from finding meaning in things you do—not the other way around.[12]

Richard has used this time to significantly improve his furniture-making abilities. This medical-device scientist and developer has also started teaching at a local university and creating beautiful furniture for his home and those of his children. He is teaching people with disabilities specific furniture-repair skills. He feels deeply about the opportunity to give back and help others. He has also rediscovered his love of music by playing his guitar and finding opportunities to perform for others. He has discovered the meaning of sharing his creativity and talents with others.

2. Will you have enough money?

This is also the time when you will assess whether you will have enough money to make it through the rest of your life. The primary issue is whether your financial resources and income-generating capabilities will pay for the expenses associated with the life you seek. Some people will work with a financial planner to assess their needs and the resources

---

[12] Friedman, Howard, PhD, and Leslie Martin, PhD, *The Longevity Project: Surprising Discovers of Health and Long Life from a Benchmark Eight-Decade Study,* Plume Publishers, 2012.

they have available. They will establish an investment philosophy that is focused more on preserving capital than realizing long-term gains. The risk orientation is lower, but they realize that their investments and returns should cover them until they are one hundred years old. They will also need to determine the expected expenses and consider which ones are fixed and which are variable. They will need to make assumptions about inflation and cost of living to anticipate their expenses over their lifetimes. Comparing income and expenses should answer the question about the fuel and what changes or controls may be needed in one's lifestyle to ensure they can afford what they want to do.

According to a study by Northwest Mutual (2018 Planning and Progress Study) of more than two thousand adults, 21 percent of Americans have nothing saved for their retirement years, and approximately 30 percent have less than $5,000. This means that a majority of Americans will rely on Social Security for their income needs. The average American is only slightly better, with having just $84,821 in their retirement savings, a number that is significantly less than the $1 million most experts believe are necessary to supplement Social Security for retirement. These numbers reinforce the belief that 78 percent of Americans say they are "somewhat" to "extremely" concerned about not having enough money for their retirement, and 66 percent believe they will outlive their savings.[13]

Integrating the available resources into what one does with their time helps create an alignment of two important elements during this stage: financial conditions and desired lifestyle.

In their long-term marriage, Toby was the saver, and David was the spender. Both held each other in check to save for their kids' college educations and their retirement and have fun throughout their lives. As they entered this next stage, they worked with a financial planner and determined that, for the most part, they should have sufficient financial resources to live the lifestyle they wanted. They still needed to be careful, and they enjoy finding creative ways to save money. The emotional hurdle Toby overcame occurred when she was out visiting an antique store and saw something she wanted. In the past, she would have moved on, but on this day, she bought it. This simple action

---

[13]   Northwestern Mutual 2018 Planning and Progress Study.

brought great satisfaction and fun. She had accomplished what she has been saving for all her life: the time to buy small things just for the fun of it and not worry or feel guilty about the financial impact. What an achievement.

3. Who do you want to live with?

The question implies that we only need to look at one relationship, but many relationships change during this stage. Many people entering this stage of life have been involved in a long-term marriage or relationship that has likely focused on building careers and raising children. Now, the children are on their own, off the "family payroll" and creating their own homes. Many couples will see this as an opportunity to renew their vows and pursue activities they have long put off together. Others will find their relationship has little meaning or emotional connection. In addition, many people have long-term, deep friendships in the workplace. Leaving the working environment changes these relationships and leaves individuals without a social community in which they have shared many challenges.

The question as you enter this next stage is how these relationships should and will change and evolve. Research has found that healthy relationships are a core characteristic of healthy and happy people. Men tend to live longer if they are in a routine, marriage-type relationship. For women, being married is not so important, but having a core group of "sisters" is highly correlated with a long and happy life. The question here is, Who is in your community? Consider the different levels of relationships you have. How important are the various relationships in your life now and in this next stage? What are you doing to create, nurture, retain, and grow them? We will explore what this means and why these are important.

4. How do you stay healthy?

Health is one thing that hangs over individuals at this stage of life and creates a great sense of uncertainty, stress, and dread. Health is vitally important because it affects what you can do during this stage of life. Choices for maintaining and retaining your health are important, and the sooner you understand what you need to do to retain your health, the better. It is important to understand what you need to do and why.

Scientific breakthroughs have made this stage of life possible. There are research efforts that are finding ways to extend life and integrate devices or replacements that enhance abilities and create new opportunities to fulfill one's wants for life. Scientists are creating medical techniques that increase the body's strength, flexibility, and resilience.

A healthy lifestyle can make a significant difference in the length of time and quality of life for individuals in all stages. This includes a wholesome diet, exercising, yoga, meditation, active sports, tai chi, and taking ten thousand steps per day. Technology has provided us with tools to measure, monitor, encourage, and motivate us to live heathy lifestyles. All of this is making significant differences in how we live and how well we live. There is much developing research and guidance for these factors, and it is important to fully understand them and incorporate them into our daily lives.

5. Who are you going to be?

When you enter this stage, you often leave behind many of the elements that defined your identity and structure to your time and interests. You are no longer going to an office or workplace. You may have a new business card that shows your name, phone, and email, but there is no job title. You pause a moment when someone asks what you do for a living. This question gets at your sense of identity and how you describe yourself to others. It also examines how you use your time, resources, relationships, and more. Your lifestyle will be a demonstration of your self-image.

When asked what you do, do you simply answer, "I'm retired"? If so, what does this mean to you and connote to the other person? This is a time when your identity is created by the things you do. This is a time where you can create the person you want to be *now*, based on a lifetime of experiences, successes, disappointments, and interests. This is a time when you can forge different daily routines that are consistent with what you want to do now. What you do with this time and how you live this next stage will truly define who you want to be. So, it is important to think about this question in a way that integrates the responses to the previous questions and provides a pathway to a meaningful life.

What is different now is that you are making the conscious choice about how you want to live your life, integrating all the elements you've realized are important, and then building this lifestyle into your daily routine. This time requires you to take the initiative and become self-motivated to pursue the things you want. This new responsibility defines in many ways how your life is different than when you were younger. As was said earlier, you have the ultimate decision and responsibility for building the life you want within the parameters of your world.

The Next Biological Clock

Individuals in this stage of life face a biological clock that is different from those in the Realizing Adulthood stage. This is a time of independence where you have successfully left work commitments, career advancement, and family obligations. There is a realization that your time on this planet is limited, and there will come a day when you will not be able to do things you want. That day may come suddenly or may come gradually. This fear, this concern, that time is more limited than in earlier periods of life serves as a motivating force to pursue, create, and engage something meaningful. Those who do not develop these skills often become depressed, soured on life, resentful, and hopeless. This is the despair syndrome that Erikson spoke about.

There is a paradox here. Individuals at this stage are both self-centered and community-centered. They are concerned about doing things they have put off for years and have experiences that deepen themselves intellectually, emotionally, and spiritually. This is also a time for giving back to others and contributing to creating change that makes this a better world. The core of this motivation is about the fulfilment of hope.

As the song quote by Tom Rush at the top of the chapter indicates, "What makes you grow old is replacing hope with regret."[14] When the hope you feel about the adventures that await is replaced with regret about the choices you made, failures you experienced, and limitations you face, the zest for life diminishes. The alternative is fear, isolation, and despair. Some will experience this, and this will become their new normal. Erikson views the challenge to find hope at this stage of life like that of a young child because they have no reference point to judge where they are. Individuals at this stage of life are living unbounded by obligations or commitments, but they have habits, expectations, relationships, and a life full of experiences, joys, and disappointments. So, this is a time for renewal, openness, and adventure to keep hope alive.

Moving from ideas and excitement about the possibilities to action and change may require building a Master Plan. This can be a simple or an in-depth plan. To be worth the time and paper, the plan should help you make commitments about things you will continue doing and things you will change. It should help you chart and reinforce the changes you are seeking. This Reinventing stage of life requires addressing critical questions.

Within each question, there are additional questions and considerations. Ignoring these issues will leave your life to chance. Are you willing to just see what happens? You are making a decision when you choose to not make a decision. Adjustments may be small or large. The chapters that follow will provide information, ideas, and stories of others for you to consider. It is simply your life—the only one you have been given—to make of it what you can and what you want.

The central challenge and skill that needs to be developed at this stage is taking command of your time and talents and employing them in a manner that creates meaning and value in your life. You will be living within the parameters of those financial considerations, relationships, and wants that define who you are. Now is the time to determine what you want and then create the life you've always wanted. Let's get started.

---

[14]   Tom Rush, "Too Many Memories" from *What I Know*.

Chapter 4

What Do You Want to Do with Your Time?

Life isn't about finding yourself; it's about creating
yourself. So, live the life you imagined.
—Henry David Thoreau

I met Tony at a Red Sox training camp game in Fort Myers, Florida. He was ninety-four years old and had played minor league baseball when he was younger. He loves baseball.

I asked, "So, Tony, what is the secret to a long life?"

He quickly replied, "Never stop working!"

We both laughed.

Then his wife leaned over and said, "And he never sits down!"

Tony and many others have discovered that being *engaged* creates a long and happy life. When I ask a question about what you want to do with your time, I am looking to understand the purpose with which you organize and live your life—and how you use your time. This goes beyond how you fill your day or your calendar, and it challenges you to understand why you are doing the things and whether they are a good use of your time. A wonderful aspect of this life stage is that you can pursue those things that are meaningful and important to you. In this chapter, we will explore how to discover your sense of purpose through a series of questions and explorations. The goal is to give you information to make critical choices and commitments so that when you are no longer able, you can look back and feel that you have lived the life you imagined.

There are several reasons for why this is important. The Longevity Project[15] identified several factors that lead to a longer life. They include "striving to accomplish your goals, setting new aims when milestones are reached, and staying engaged and productive." Friedman and Martin conclude that hard work increases life expectancy rather than causing stress and shortening it. Maintaining engagement in the world is what is shown to be most critical to a happy, meaningful, and extended life.

At Harvard University, Robert Waldinger led a study on aging:

> The people who seem happiest are the people who feel like they're able to express aspects of themselves that feel vital to them, that make them feel alive. It's not any particular path you have taken, it's being able to express the core of who you are.[16]

The benefits of a purposeful focus to life can be significant. According to David Bennett at Rush University Medical Center and a leader of the Nun Study on Aging, people operating with a sense of purpose have more fluid and flexible brains. They are able to tolerate pressures because they have ways of dealing with issues that people without a sense of purpose don't have. Older people who scored high on having a sense of purpose in life were twice as likely to live longer over the five-year study as those who scored low.[17]

In another study, the MIDUS Project at the University of Wisconsin, Carol Ryff, chief scientist, studied more than seven thousand people and their brains from ages twenty-five to seventy-four.[18] The factors that led to higher levels of health and happiness were:

---

[15]   Friedman, Howard, PhD, and Leslie Martin, PhD, *The Longevity Project: Surprising Discovers of Health and Long Life from a Benchmark Eight-Decade Study*, Plume Publishers, 2012.

[16]   Harvard Second Generation Study, www.adultdevelopmentstudy.org.

[17]   Riley, K. P., Snowdon, D. A., Desrosiers M. F., Markesbery W. R., "Early life linguistic ability, late life cognitive function, and neuropathology: Findings from the Nun Study Neurobiology of Aging," 26(3):341347, 2005.

[18]   www.midus.wisc.edu/.

- a sense of purpose in life, of direction for the rest of one's life
- autonomy and the independence to control one's own behavior and not looking to others for approval
- mastery over one's environment, with the ability to create or choose environments where they could thrive
- self-acceptance and knowing one's own strengths and weaknesses
- personal growth and seeking meaning, learning, and sense of evolving
- positive relations with other people

In addition, a *Lancet* study followed nine thousand people over the age of sixty-five and found that those with a higher sense of purpose and belief that life has meaning were less likely to die in the next eight and a half years than those who did not share these beliefs. Their correlations held even when the researchers controlled for other demographic factors, mental and physical health, age, and gender. There is a clear sense that well-being and health are closely related to individuals with a strong sense of purpose, meaning, and appreciation with life conditions.[19]

These studies demonstrate clearly that living a purposeful life, one where you are engaged and feel a sense of importance for how you spend your time, leads to remarkable value for you. Purpose, according to Richard Leider, author of *The Power of Purpose*, is the "active expression of the deepest dimensions within us, where we have a profound sense of who we are and why we're here. Purpose is the aim around which we structure our lives, source for direction and energy. Through the lenses of purpose, we are able to see ourselves—our future—more clearly."[20]

Aristotle (384–322 BC) believed that each person had a sense of purpose, that it only needed to be uncovered, and that the function of life is to fulfill this purpose. He believed this purpose can be achieved through reason and the acquisition of virtue. He also believed that each individual should use his or her talents to their fullest potential. Happiness is realized through the full exercise of these abilities. People

---

[19]   Steptoe, Andrew, Deaton, A., Stone, A. A., "Subjective wellbeing, health and ageing," Series, *Lancet*, 2015: 385:640–48, November 14, 2014.

[20]   Leider, Richard, *The Power of Purpose: Find Meaning, Live Longer, Better*, Barrett-Koehler Publisher, Oakland, CA, 2015.

take pride in what they do. He encourages us to seek to understand truth, pursue a moral existence, and promote our ideals in the world through action.

We need to define purpose as not something to fill your daily calendar or as lofty goals or activities. Finding your purpose is not just about pursuing a new career or getting engaged in some major social change or social mission-type activity; it is finding those things that give you personal meaning, satisfaction, and joy. Many people use this time to focus on playing golf or spending more time with the grandchildren. Many people learn or relearn a musical instrument, work in their tool shed, or seek adventures in other lands. Some are working through their bucket lists and addressing gaps they've long lived with. Are they not purpose driven?

While I value and appreciate the importance of having a sense of mission and purpose in life, I also believe it is important to discover what engages you, nourishes you, and provides meaning to your life—even though it may not involve changing the world. For others, changing the world or volunteering in a school system is just what is needed to fill the gap. This stage gives us the opportunity to discover what we want to do with our lives and determine what is important to us. When considering what is important during this stage of his life, John L., one if the individuals interviewed for this book, identified the importance of letting go of the need to fill one's calendar. "I want to replace achievement with purpose and pursuit of satisfaction. I want to feel more *being* oriented as opposed to *doing* oriented."

It may be difficult to let go of things that brought you professional satisfaction. You received a sense of accomplishment, a feeling that you were valued for something, a view that you were important. Work provides many things beyond a paycheck. It provides a place to go in the morning, things that are important and must get done, a feeling of progress and accomplishment, and a strong social network of colleagues and friends. You feel like you are plugged into the world and that things you did—or other people did—matter. When one leaves the workplace, these attributes of life are left behind. What can replace them? What can give your life meaning when there is less time left in your life but more free time during the day? If ever there was a time when you can choose what to do and when to do it, now is that time.

Discovering Your Passions and Energy Sources

There are several ways to discover your purpose and determine the things you need to pursue during this next stage. We will start by understanding where your energy comes from and the actions that attract your passions. To discover your energy sources, you do not need to look further than what you have done in your past. In your career or life history, there were times when you experienced a profound sense of who you are and why you're here. This experience provided you with an amazing sense of energy, clarity, and fulfillment. So, to find your purpose, let's start there.

In *Flow: The Psychology of Optimal Experience*,[21] Mihaly Csikszentmihalyi provides a powerful description of the "flow" and what it means to the individual. Think of a time when you were doing something that you truly loved, where time seemed to fly by. When you were in your zone, you were doing things that gave you great satisfaction and renewed energy. When you were done with those tasks, you felt more energized than before. The tasks engaged you intensely, and the work seemed so natural. Others may comment on how you made this work look so easy or how much harder it would have been for them to do, but for you, it is easy, enjoyable, and fulfilling. The work may have been challenging, but you loved the challenge. You would love to spend more time doing things like this, and now, at this stage of your life, you can.

In the box below, write down the answers to the questions. Describe the times and activities when you were in your zone. There are likely to be many. Write down a few important ones. This may go far back in your life or career or have occurred in the past few months. The important lesson here is to understand what it was about these experiences that

---

[21]   Csikszentmihalyi, Mihaly, *Flow: The Psychology of Optimal Experience*, Harper Perennial Modern Classics, New York, 2008.

gave you energy, joy, excitement, fulfillment, and passion. This is the best time to discover or rediscover these life forces within you.

> In the space below, describe 3 or 4 times when you felt you were truly "in your zone." You greatly enjoyed what you were doing and felt enriched, energized and engaged by the experience. What were you doing? Where were you? Why was this experience important to you?

1

2

3

4

5

Find the Guideposts

As you look at what you wrote down (hopefully you could relive the feelings you had during those times), it is important to understand the underlying motivations that were moving within you. Then, as you move forward in the next stage, you will be able to determine whether these same motivations exist within you and can form a foundation for determining how you want to spend your time. This can be done by identifying the common themes that defined what you sought or avoided. You can think of these as career or life guideposts. These are attributes of your life experiences that describe the type of activities you are drawn to and require little external encouragement. You just love doing them. They are the things that attracted you to a job, role, or activity. They may be conscious, known, or they may be instinctual or unknown at the time. The reasons should become clear now. You will know them because you have been drawn to them or guided by how these forces shape your experiences and interests.

There are many frameworks to use in identifying these guideposts. A helpful framework is to see your life path in terms of one or a combination of the following guideposts. Which one (or ones) sounds like you? Select one or two and rate them high, medium, or low in relation to how important they are to you then and now.

1) Achievement

Your professional or life experiences—the times when you were in your zone—gave you a sense of accomplishment with important goals or objectives. You progressed in your chosen profession, organization, or life's work. You look back on what you have done and feel a strong sense of pride about what you have achieved or received. You have met challenges and were successful.

2) Leadership

Your professional or life experiences—the times when you were in your zone—gave you an opportunity to exercise leadership. You are proud of how well you led a team or organization. What they did was important, and they could not have done that without your leadership. Regardless of the size, you have been their captain, boss, person in charge, guide, facilitator, or leader. Your life experience can be characterized by growth, development, and accomplishment as a leader.

3) Helping Others

In your professional or life experiences—the times when you were in your zone—you made a difference to others. In your own way, what you have done has made a serious, important, and positive impact in the lives of the people your work has touched. Because of you, their lives are different and better than they would have been had you not been there. The work you have done has made an important contribution to their well-being.

4) Relationships

Your professional or life experiences—the times when you were in your zone—were defined by collaboration and the relationships you have made with others. You enjoy working with others in a team, group, or organization. You can easily name the colleagues with whom you have worked, and in these experiences, you may have developed lasting friendships. As you look back on your life experience and the times when you were fully engaged, you always seem to be working in close teams. You are drawn to them. These are important to you regardless of the work itself. You clearly believe that work is best done through the collaborative efforts of people.

5) Personal Creativity and Growth

In your professional or life experiences – the times when you were in your zone – provided you with an opportunity to learn something new or different, and you were deepened personally. You continually seek to stretch yourself, learn and understand elements in you, and get better at what you love doing. Your work or experiences in your zone engaged your creativity and your inherent ability to solve problems, create something, and use innovative thinking. You love performing your unique talents for others. When you have created something, you feel enriched and enlightened—and deep sense of satisfaction at what was done.

6) Making the World a Better Place

In your professional or life experiences, you made a positive difference difference to the world. You hope the work you did reached well beyond those immediately impacted or has somehow changed the conditions or experiences of others. You felt a sense of mission through this work.

You may find that several guideposts have defined your life experience. Try to determine the one or two that have been the most important to you. Can you describe the type of experiences that give you the greatest meaning and why? These are the experiences that enrich, engage, and sustain you.

Discovering Your Unique Abilities

This discovery task is helpful for understanding where your sense of energy, passion, and joy come from. During this Reinventing stage, you may want to replicate these experiences. It is important, however, to look beyond the tasks and discover your unique abilities. As you think about what you accomplished and experienced when you were in your zone, you most likely employed some unique skills and abilities. To determine how to spend your time, you may find it useful to identify the attributes, skills, and competencies that helped you be successful. When you look for new activities, you can find those that utilize these unique abilities in effective ways.

Some refer to these as strengths, gifts, talents, or competencies. These are the unique abilities that each person has that help make them successful in work, relationships, and general living. These strengths are the foundation and building blocks of a successful career and life experience. When one is doing the things they love, they fully utilize their strengths, and motivation is never an issue. In this stage of life, doing what one enjoys, seeks to learn more, and builds on what one does well leads to a more fulfilling and meaningful life experience.[22] Consequently, it is important to understand these strengths, these core competencies, and integrate them into your Master Plan. Perhaps you can find opportunities to develop these strengths even further.

There are several credible methods and well-researched models for identifying one's unique abilities. The leading ones in my view are described below. While most of these frameworks are usually applied to the workplace, it is relatively easy to translate them to identify your own characteristics and the things that make you successful in whatever pursuit you choose for this reinventing stage of life. Your task is to select one (or several) of these methods and use it (or them) to identify your true unique abilities. There is a brief description of the various tools, and links to the resources are provided below.

1) StrengthsFinder

In the early 1950s, Donald O. Clifton noticed that much of the research in psychology focused on mental illnesses. He decided to explore the attributes of successful people. Over the next five decades, he and his colleagues at the Gallup Organization developed a model for identifying the characteristics of successful people. Because people, situations, and definitions of success have many interpretations, they developed this research into their StrengthsFinder model. In their work, they developed an assessment tool that includes thirty-four areas of talent.

When you complete the assessment tool, their report will show you the top five strengths that are characteristic of you. Then, there are a number of books and other resource materials you can acquire from them to further understand your strengths, the research behind this model, and tools for employing these strengths in your work,

---

[22]   Harzer, C., & Ruch, W. (2012). "When the job is a calling: The role of applying one's signature strengths at work," *The Journal of Positive Psychology*, 7, 362–371.

life, or next stage settings. This information can be found at www.strengthsfinder.com

2) VIA Institute of Character

The VIA Institute is a nonprofit organization focused on helping people identify their hidden strengths. This work was based on the research work of Dr. Martin Seligman. He was known as the "father of positive psychology" and is the author of several books and research papers on the power of positive psychology.

The VIA survey tool is regarded as a central assessment guide to help people understand their unique abilities. They have identified twenty-four characteristics in their research. Their survey assessment instrument will help identify your five most dominant characteristics. This survey instrument and the research work that underlies its development can be found at www.viacharacter.org.

3) Gardner's Intelligences

In the early 1980s Howard Gardner, professor and researcher at Harvard University, developed a framework for understanding eight different intelligences (multiple intelligences) of people.[23] Each individual has multiple strengths, and the value is discovering which ones are most characteristic of you. There is no comparable assessment tool for these intelligences. These intelligences describe those life activities that reflect core competencies and show different patterns of interest and skill. More information can be found at www.howardgardner.com.

4) Strong Interest Inventory

Psychologist Edward Strong Jr. developed a test to determine people's career interests back in 1927. It has since been updated, refined, and recalibrated to address more current research and frameworks on career

---

[23] Gardner, Howard, *Multiple Intelligences: New Horizons in Theory and Practice*, Basic Books Publisher, 2006.

planning. It has been revised by Jo-Ida Hansen and David Campbell and most recently by John Holland. The purpose of the assessment tool is to provide insights into areas that may be of interest or importance to people's careers. It is used by many psychologists and career counselors to assist their clients and determine what areas are suitable for their careers. While the assessment and resulting guidance are primarily focused on individuals seeking a job or career, it can provide helpful information for determining the kinds of activities one may focus their next stage time and talents. The Strong Interest Inventory can provide the individual with information and insights on specific areas of work and leisure activities. There are multiple sources for this information and the assessment tools. A suggested one is www.careerassessmentsite.com.

Once you are comfortable with the list of your strengths, review and discuss them with individuals who are close to you and get their feedback. It is important to test these characteristics and determine whether your perception of yourself is consistent with how others see you. There are no right or wrong answers, but there are interpretations and value received from learning about yourself. The important outcome from these tasks is to understand your strengths and true talents on a deeper level. The challenge now is finding ways to employ these unique abilities in the things that really matter to you.

At this point in the process, you have examined the times when you were in your zone and the guideposts that influenced your career and life experiences. You assessed, identified, and tested your set of strengths, talents, and unique abilities. Hopefully, you have learned much about yourself and gained new insights. These insights should enhance what you already know about yourself and provide important references for identifying what you want to do in this next stage of your life.

Creating Your Bucket List

Looking back on life can be both exciting and discouraging. You see what you have accomplished and the times when you felt highly successful. It can also be discouraging because you see things you did not finish, did not achieve, or were not successful at. Part of this process of discovering purpose and planning for your next stage of life will be to identify things you want to do and let go of the things that no longer matter. There are two types of items for your bucket list (things you want to do before you "kick the bucket"). There are things you would like to do again and things you have never done but want to. This list is something you can have fun with and integrate into your Master Plan for this next stage. At this point, you are not making commitments to do any of them, but they do reflect things that are on your mind now. This list may be long, short, or something you'll need to develop over time. We will be developing and refining this list in chapter 9, and this will be important for figuring out your priorities and making changes in your life.

Identifying and Accepting Your Constraints

As you look at the activities that give you energy and things you want to do in this next stage, it is also very important to understand the limitations. You may be thinking, *Yes, I'd really like to do these things, but …*

While I speak often about the freedom you have to make your own choices at this life stage, you may have certain constraints or responsibilities that limit what you can honestly pursue. It is important to understand them and incorporate them into the course you set for yourself.

Some of these constraints are temporary, and others are permanent. Some of these will be responsibilities that you chose to live with, and others have been or will be thrust upon you. While one may not want to care for aging parents or troubled children, you may believe it is your responsibility to do so. No one ever promised that this period of life is not without limitations or constraints. The important message here is to understand them, accept them, find creative ways to optimize the value of this time, and appreciate the value you provide to this person.

It is important to understand the nature of these constraints and realize you will need to be more creative and resourceful than others to fulfill your own wants. The limitations may be based on financial considerations (income or expenses) that may impact or require resources or changes to your current financial situation. You simply cannot afford to do those things you want to do. You may need to keep earning income and living simply. We will explore this more deeply in the next chapter.

The limitations may be because of your responsibilities to current relationships. Would doing something on your bucket or want list cause pain or trouble in relationships that are important to you. Consider how certain actions would affect or change your relationships. While we will explore the nature of your relationships in a later chapter, it is important to understand and assess the impact of your actions on your relationships. You may be surprised that you have a willing partner. You might not be able to move forward because the relationship is more important than the idea of something you want to do.

You may have requirements or challenges because of your physical abilities. Would you need to acquire significantly more skill than you have now? Are there other reasons why this is difficult or challenging? Do you believe you can do this? At this stage of life, you are likely to have more physical limitations than when you were younger. Depending on what you want to do, you can examine whether the desired tasks require physical abilities that you frankly do not have or cannot create without significant cost or effort. It is important to understand, accept, and appreciate these limitations.

Embrace Your Sense of Purpose

In *Composing a Further Life*, Mary Catherine Bateson shares remarkable insights on this time of life.[24] As we ask ourselves, "Who am I?" or "Am I still the person I have spent my lifetime becoming?" Bateson points out that we face a choice of where to put our efforts. Do we continue to learn as we get older? Do we seek to find a new consciousness and new forms of commitment, acquiring new skills? She points out that one of the strengths of the American culture is the belief that we can reinvent ourselves, but one of the weaknesses is our willingness to discard earlier learnings. Through this process of discovery, it is important to look at

---

[24] Bateson, Mary Catherine, *Composing a Further Life*, Vintage Publishers, 2011.

your experiences, learn from what you have done in the past, and see what guides you about what you want to do now that you have time, freedom, and curiosity.

John L. has been a professor at a private college for many years and is in the process of moving away from that work. He has served on several boards of private organizations, primarily nonprofit, and this is where he feels engaged. He enjoys dealing with governance and organizational design issues that will impact the lives and work of these organizations. As he creates more time in his schedule, he is filling it with more governance development work with organizations he truly appreciates.

Patricia has worked for a city government for many years. She has worked in most departments, and she loves what she does. The work is part politician, part administrator, and part problem-solver of real-world community development. She is in her midseventies and is going strong. She doesn't know when or how she will stop working, but she likes the flexibility they have given her about her schedule and the level of respect she has achieved from her coworkers and the community. Her reinventing stage is filled with work she enjoys.

Randy was a physical education teacher for more than thirty-five years. After his early retirement from teaching, he tried many things, but he basically became bored. He remembered and rediscovered how much he loved coaching kids and working with them to build their self-esteem. He is in his element when he is in the classroom and the gym. He has translated this insight and his energy into being an assistant coach and helping the other coaches discover the joy of working with growing children. He is getting involved in a leadership role with a regional association that promotes the sport. He also discovered a creative talent for painting landscapes. At seventy-five, his life is full of time with friends, teaching, and expressing his creative self. Randy is fully engaged in many activities and enjoys time with his girlfriend and their friends.

In his twenties, Tom was an avid white-water canoeist. Because of work, children, and family commitments, he put away his paddles and life jacket. Whenever he saw a river, he would analyze and plan precisely how to navigate the rapids. After he turned sixty and the kids were gone, he took a class in Maine for white-water kayaking. It was just what he wanted. He learned a lot, was challenged to the brink, and relived the experiences of his youth. When asked by other members of the class to join in more trips, he said no. He was done and could now leave this want and move on to other adventures. He thought it would be his new passion, but after this experiment, he realized that his interests would be found elsewhere.

An important concept to remember is that time is *not* on your side. You have more limited time on this planet than when you were younger. This is the time to do something about your life so that when you look back at some point, you can see that you have finished the unfinished items and resolved the outstanding items in your life. This is a time to discover and bring those elements that give true meaning to your life. It is a time to identify and utilize your unique abilities. It is a time to do those things you've always wanted to do but put off because of work, family commitments, or worries about the future. It is a time to recognize, accept, and adjust your life to the constraints of your life. It is time to establish clear priorities, and as Thoreau said, "Live the life you imagined."

Chapter 5
Will You Have Enough Money?

A nickel ain't worth a dime anymore.
—**Yogi Berra**

Money—and figuring out how much you will need—is a complex issue because it is analytical and emotional, present and future focused, tangible and uncertain. It is often uncomfortable to deal with these issues, but it is essential to fully understand and integrate the conclusions into your lifestyle. It is also vitally important to have the conversations with your spouse or partner so that you agree on the core decisions and understand your present and future financial conditions. The outcome should provide the clarity and confidence you need to utilize your assets and live the life you feel you have earned and want. The alternative is to avoid these conditions and then leave to chance or face undesired consequences at the time when you will be least able to make adjustments. Your goal of this analysis should be to add this information to your Master Plan and integrate the actions that create the life you want. Hopefully, your concerns about your financial condition will fall into the background and you can pursue your future life. Before we get there, we will look at this issue in a serious, thoughtful, and systematic manner.

This chapter will not provide investment advice or specific formulas for how much you will have or need. We will examine information that should help you prepare for and work with a financial planner. You may already know much of the information—or it may be irrelevant given your personal financial situation. I have tried to cover a broad scope of considerations and provide information that will help you understand why and where certain guidance comes from. This chapter will help you understand a variety of the concepts, principles, and techniques for assessing and planning actions that will help you make the most of your financial resources.

Choose Your Financial Planner Wisely

Your financial advisor can be an independent expert or a full-service organization that provides a variety of services, including financial planning, tax preparation, investment management, and trust and estate management. It is critical that your financial advisors work as a team for your benefit and the benefit of your heirs. They should earn their fees from serving your interests and what you want for your family—current and future. There are many charming, attractive, and effective scams in the market for your money. There are also people who are legitimate and provide a valuable service but may provide you with more than what you need and reap an inappropriate financial benefit from your buying decisions. They may sell you more than what you really need. However, there are also many highly competent, caring, and high-integrity financial advisors. Your task is to choose wisely. So, follow a process that leads you to the right person where you don't need to worry about your financial well-being and can focus on the other important priorities of your life.

There are basically five types of financial advisors or service providers.

1) Insurance Agent

This is an individual who is licensed to sell various forms of insurance, including life, disability, long-term care, and annuities, and is usually paid based on the size of the products you buy. Their interests may or may not be aligned with your needs, but when you need one of these products, you will likely work with one of these advisors. They can provide a valuable service.

2) Registered Representative

This is an individual who sells investment products. She or he is licensed to sell securities (stocks, bonds, mutual funds, and so forth) and is often referred to as a stockbroker. They work on commissions based on the size and type of transactions they do for you.

3) Registered Investment Advisor

This is an individual who provides investment advice and manages investments. He or she is aligned with your goals and risk orientation. They usually charge a management fee based on a percent of the assets they manage. For example, if you have $1 million in investments, and they charge 1 percent management fee, you will pay them $10,000 per year to manage your assets. They may provide other services (like tax preparation) as part of this fee or as an extra-charge service.

4) Bank Representative or Trust Advisor

This is an individual who is employed by a bank or financial institution and manages your assets and estate. She or he works with you to set financial goals and handles everything from managing your investments, providing you with regular income (like an allowance), or paying the monthly bills for you and/or your family. They work for the financial institution who charges you a fee like an investment advisor.

5) Financial Planner

This is an individual who seeks to understand your situation and develop a plan to address the objectives you have. They will develop a total financial strategy and plan and help you with certain transactions. They may look at your insurance, wills, and estate documents and assist you in getting what you need. Their compensation is based on an hourly fee or a service fee. This covers their time, expertise, and any tools they use while developing and tracking your financial results. These individuals should be professionally licensed as a certified financial planner (CFP). Their primary role is as a planner; any transactions may need the services of one of the other roles described above, and the fees for these services are additional.

While professional and technical competence is a critical selection criterion, how you feel, how well they understand what you want, their understanding of your particular circumstances, and their commitment to your success are also important. To find the right one, use referrals from friends or trusted advisors (attorney, banker, etc.). Take time to interview several and assess them against your selection criteria.

When Les and his wife were selecting their financial planner, he realized that selecting someone who they could work with and trust, who understood what they wanted, and who would be responsive to their requests was critical. It took several meetings to select the particular firm and individual, but they realized the importance of this extra effort. Remember, however, that you are ultimately responsible for your own financial well-being.

Determine How Much You Will Have (Your Income)

Perhaps one of the most important steps will be the time when your income shifts from what you earn to what you receive from your assets. At this point, you will start living off what you have created through your working stages of life, and your earned income will become a lesser and lesser amount of your monthly income, until it is completely stops. Therefore, it is important to understand the different sources of income you have available to you. This will likely have a major impact on what you can do for the remainder of your life.

There are basically five sources of income.

1) Earned Income

This is income one receives from working. This may come from a current job, perhaps with fewer hours and less income than when one was employed full-time. This may be another job or income-producing activity in this stage of life. It is usually taxed through withholdings or with estimated tax filings you do quarterly.

2) Social Security or Public Pension

This is income received from the government for American citizens who have paid into the system. Most other countries have similar programs. Some individuals who worked in the public sector and did not pay into the federal Social Security program in their working life will not be eligible for Social Security income. They will likely have a similar program provided by the federal, state, or local government entity or school system for which they worked. Also, it is often wise for many individuals to wait to start their Social Security payments until they reach age seventy. While you may be eligible at sixty-two, holding off till later years has a very strong impact on the income you will receive in the later years. The amount you will receive increases by approximately 6.5–8 percent per year, so it is like getting an 8 percent raise to your income each year until you reach age seventy. For example, Karen's social security income would be $990 per month if she took this at age sixty-five, but it would $1,365 if she waits till she is seventy years old. To determine your projected income, visit the Social Security website (www.ssa.gov/planners/benefitcalculators).

3) Private Pension or Annuity Income

Few organizations provide pensions or annuity benefits, so if you have one, consider yourself lucky. In the US, the number of employees eligible to receive pensions has declined from 63 percent in 1983 to 17 percent in 2013.[25] This is income one receives on a monthly or quarterly basis that is tied to a previous investment made by one's former employer or investments made to generate an annuity. This stream of income may be fixed or have some variable feature that increases with inflation. The

---

[25]   Gratton, Lynda and Andrew Scott, *The 100-Year Life: Living and Working in an Age of Longevity*, Bloomsbury Business Publications, New York, 2017.

solvency of the employer or annuity provider is essential and is likely guaranteed by the Department of Labor (Employee Benefits Security Administration). If this is an important source of income for you, check to validate the solvency of the organization and terms of this income source. This will help you sleep better knowing what income is likely to be received from this source for the remainder of your life (and possibly your spouse's life.)

4) Investment Income

This is the income that is generated from your assets or investments. This may be earned as dividends, interest paid to bond holders, rental income from income-producing properties, royalty income for patents, inventions, leases, or books, or gains received when you sell stock or mutual funds. One's home is usually not considered an asset for investment income unless it is generating income from rental or property use. Using the home as an income asset will be discussed later. Finally, this includes any money you consider savings, however it is held, to provide for future living expenses. Many people built up these investment accounts through contributions made to retirement accounts, such as an IRA, Roth IRA, or a 401(k) or 403(b) plan at work. The dollars were invested on a pretax basis, but when you pull them out, they are taxed as ordinary income (much like a salary). Further, currently the IRS requires individuals who reach seventy and a half to start withdrawing from their tax-deferred retirement accounts. This is called the Required Minimum Distribution (RMD). The amount depends on the amount and one's age. The intention here is to make sure you receive the taxable income at a rate that enables the government to receive income taxes from your deferred compensation. At age seventy, this withdrawal rate is approximately 3.7 percent, and it increases to 5.4 percent at age eighty. You can determine this amount by asking the Internal Revenue Service (www.irs.gov/retirement-plans/plan-participant-employee/retirement-topics-required-minimum-distributions-rmds).

5) Sale of Assets or Receipts of an Inheritance

This is income that is generated when you sell a house, vacation home, or investment property or other assets that may or may not be generating income or receive a lump-sum payment from the death of a family member. This can include utilizing the cash value generated within a whole-life or universal life insurance policy or other income within deferred compensation plans established when one was working. Once you sell (or receive) the asset, it becomes a more accessible asset and may become a source for investment income as described above.

There are many factors that impact the income generated from investments. Your earned income may be reduced when you are no longer able or interested in working. However, many individuals continue working for pay because this is what gives them meaning and challenge and a feeling of making a contribution to the world. Social Security or other secured income sources may increase slightly in relation to the cost of living or inflation. However, one should be cautious to not plan on much increase here. Pension income may increase for inflation if this is included in the plan. Investment income or tangible assets (property) and the value of one's assets are the only area where one is likely to see increases in value. Since your expenses are going to increase with inflation, you need to find investments or income sources that will increase as well.

Predicting the Growth of Your Assets

You may have little in savings or invested assets or you may have multiple millions that are professionally managed. This section of the chapter will examine how to consider the growth in your assets as they are invested and the importance of timing and careful management of these assets. They are the primary source of income for many people in the future, so it is very important to be thoughtful about your assumptions and projections for their growth. Obviously, working with a financial planner will be very valuable, and he or she can help you understand your situation.

Predicting or planning for a certain growth in investments is very important and challenging. From 1900 to 2016, the Standard & Poor's

500 largest companies increased in value by 6.55 percent per year (adjusted for inflation). In another study of the market performance from 1950 to 2016, the stock market rose an average of 7.47 percent per year. This is in comparison to a 2.4 percent increase in the value of bonds and a 1.2 percent increase in the value of gold. These increases are after adjusting for inflation. Real estate provided a return that was less than 1 percent. During that time, there were major swings in the growth and decline in the overall stock market—and perhaps even more if one invested in a specific company. We all know that past performance is no predictor of future performance. There are many factors that lead to positive returns on investments, and those that seek to beat the market are most often beaten by the market. It will be important to establish an amount of increase that is realistic, and conservative based on the types of assets you have. This is why assets that are diversified and balanced to your investment goals and acceptable levels of risk are important and a primary responsibility of your investment advisor and you.

Let's examine the stock market in the recent past. The S&P 500 stock index between 1998 and 2018 experienced the following fluctuations:

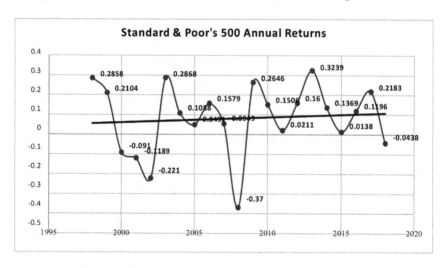

Over this time period (1998–2018), the stock market produced average annual gains of only 8.2 percent. This chart shows the volatility of the stock market. The challenge is the market conditions when you need to sell investments to generate the income you need. If you needed to withdraw 4 percent from your investments in 2002, 2008, or 2018, your investment nest egg would have been seriously reduced. If you took 4 percent from the assets in 1998, 2003, 2009, or 2013, this withdrawal would have had a minor impact on the value of your assets. Consequently, the timing for withdrawing from one's investments is a very important element in determining what dollars will be available to support one's desired lifestyle for the future. Again, a financial advisor should help you with these decisions. She or he will caution you not to sell when the market tumbles and to rebalance your assets when the market has grown rapidly.

Managing the Withdrawal of Your Assets

One of the critical challenges of this stage of life is that time is not on your side. If you were in your early thirties and had most of your assets invested in the stock market, you have time to recover if there is a significant drop in the equities market as was experienced in 2008–2009. If this happens when you are in your seventies, you may need to cut back on your expenses because your assets are lower. A fixed-dollar withdrawal would be a higher percentage of the total assets than under normal conditions. If you continue to draw from this income source at the same rate, you will likely reduce your assets to a point where you will no longer have the income you need to live. Your savings may not be sufficient to carry you through. At the same time, people in this Reinventing stage may live twenty or thirty or possibly forty years, which from an investment perspective, is long-term. The challenge is to use (reduce) as little of your core assets as possible so you can be confident about having the income needed to meet everyday living expenses and use these assets if needed to meet catastrophic health-related expenses or expenses rated to moving into an assisted-living center. The risks and consequences for people in this stage are greater than for those who are younger.

The solution to this risk is to maintain your assets balanced between investment in equities, bonds, and fixed-income or cash-related products. You may want to retain one to five years of your projected living expenses in income-based investments (like bonds and cash) and use this to meet living expenses in the case of a downturn, thereby preventing you from liquidating your equity investments when they are significantly depressed. The amount could also be based on your required minimum distribution. In downturns, bonds generally hold their investment strength and can be used to meet living expenses while producing greater returns than money just kept in cash or certificates of deposit. However, their value may be volatile. One needs to find the right balance between security and opportunity that provides for the income you need and enables you to not feel stressed regardless of the economic conditions of the marketplace. Care must be taken to continue to monitor and rebalance your assets depending on market conditions.

There are practical strategies for addressing fluctuations in the market and preserving income needed for the future. For example, Dick takes three years of needed income and puts this sum into a cash or fixed-asset investment. Then, he takes the balance of his investments and puts them into the equity stock market. If one examines the history of the stock market, even when there is a major decline, the time to return to normal growth is seldom more than two or three years. During this time, Dick uses his cash to meet his income needs and thereby does not use his invested assets. When the market is down, he can wait until it returns to a normal trading range before making any withdrawals from his invested assets. Then he replenishes his cash holdings, rebalances his assets, and retains three years of living expenses in cash. The balance is invested in long-term equities. He calculates the dollars to be held based on his projected living expenses, less other sources of current income.

In *How to Make Your Money Last*, Jane Bryant Quinn recommends retaining two years of expenses in cash or money-market types of investments in order to avoid having to liquidate investment assets during down market times.[26]

---

[26]   Quinn, Jane Bryant, *How to Make Your Money Last: The Indispensable Retirement Guide*, Simon and Schuster Publishers, New York, 2016.

Withdrawal Guidelines: The 4 Percent Rule

A landmark study on determining the amount one could use from invested assets was conducted in 1998 by Cooley, Hubbard, and Walz. The Trinity study[27] concluded that if one has assets invested at 65 percent in equity and 35 percent in fixed income, then a withdrawal rate of 4 percent per year should provide sustainable income for the individual's life (this projection is based on a thirty-year time frame for withdrawing assets). This is the source of the 4 percent rule used in financial planning.

This study was again examined using a Monte Carlo analysis.[28] The findings of this study showed that a 4 percent withdrawal rate was sustainable if the investment portfolio was balanced with 50 percent in stocks, 40 percent in bonds, and 10 percent in treasury bills (or fixed income). There have been other studies with similar conclusions. The key finding is that the asset allocation of the investments has a major impact on whether 4 percent would be sustainable. Investments that were more secure, with treasury bills or bonds, were not likely to provide the sustainable income growth from investments with a 4 percent withdrawal rate. This is because the rate of return from a highly conservative investment approach would not provide enough returns to cover the dollars withdrawn, and this would result in a higher rate of asset depletion. So, the challenge is finding the right balance of investments that provide the desired income and is sufficiently conservative to preserve your assets to help you feel secure about your income.

An alternative model was developed by Blackrock Investments LLC. The model is called CoRI and provides a factor that adjusts to your age and total assets. By applying (dividing) the factor by the amount of assets you hold, the CoRI model will show you how much you can withdraw from your assets to cover your income over your expected lifetime.

---

[27] Cooley, Philip L., Carl M. Hubbard, and Daniel T. Walz. 1998. "Retirement Savings: Choosing a Withdrawal Rate That Is Sustainable," *AAII Journal*, 10, 3: 16–21.

[28] Pfau, Wade and David Blanchett, "Can Retirees Still Use a 4 percent Withdrawal Rate?, *Advisor Perspectives*, September 2, 2014.

For example, if you are sixty-five, the CoRI number is 20.29. If you have $1,000,000 in assets, then you may withdraw $49,285 annually as income from these investments ($1,000,000 ÷ 20.29 = $49,285). This is 4.9 percent of your original assets. The CoRI number varies by age (higher if you are younger or older because of your income opportunity when you are younger and life expectancy when you are older) and can be applied to whatever level of current assets you own. Overall the average income generated (or withdrawn) from this model is 5.7 percent of the assets. More information can be obtained by visiting their website at www.blackrock.com/cori-retirement-income-planning.

The following table shows the annual dollars that can be withdrawn based on different age levels and total invested retirement assets using the CoRI methodology. The CoRI factor is shown for each age level. The dollar amount is calculated by dividing this factor into different levels of total current retirement assets.

AGE	CoRI Factor	Total Current Retirement Assets				
		$100,000	$250,000	$500,000	$1,000,000	$2,500,000
60	18.37	$5,444	$13,609	$27,218	$54,437	$136,091
61	19.05	$5,249	$13,123	$26,247	$52,493	$131,234
62	19.74	$5,066	$12,665	$25,329	$50,659	$126,646
63	20.45	$4,890	$12,225	$24,450	$48,900	$122,249
64	21.08	$4,744	$11,860	$23,719	$47,438	$118,596
65	20.29	$4,929	$12,321	$24,643	$49,285	$123,213
66	19.72	$5,071	$12,677	$25,355	$50,710	$126,775
67	19.13	$5,227	$13,068	$26,137	$52,274	$130,685
68	18.53	$5,397	$13,492	$26,983	$53,967	$134,916
69	17.93	$5,577	$13,943	$27,886	$55,772	$139,431
70	17.33	$5,770	$14,426	$28,852	$57,703	$144,259
71	16.72	$5,981	$14,952	$29,904	$59,809	$149,522
72	16.11	$6,207	$15,518	$31,037	$62,073	$155,183
73	15.49	$6,456	$16,139	$32,279	$64,558	$161,394
74	14.88	$6,720	$16,801	$33,602	$67,204	$168,011

Finally, any returns you receive from your investments will likely be taxed at both the federal and state level. It is beyond the scope of this chapter to provide an overview of the tax regulations, but there are some important factors to consider. First, income you receive that has been deferred, such as what was put into a 401(k), 403(b), or similar plan will be taxed at ordinary income tax rates. Second, income that is generated from invested assets usually is subject to capital gains tax rates, which are generally lower than ordinary income taxes. Third, dollars you utilize that are based on a loan on an asset (such as a home equity loan or a whole or universal life insurance) is not taxable. You need to consider the amount of your taxes when projecting your income so that you are utilizing after-tax dollars to meet your living expenses. Again, a financial advisor should help you determine what is likely to be available from the most tax-efficient sources of income.

Other Sources of Income

If one is intending to use their house as an investment income asset, then a reverse mortgage should be examined. These programs are being marketed by many financial institutions. A reverse mortgage is similar to a home equity credit line, but rather than using the money when needed, you receive payments (monthly or quarterly) based on the equity value of your home (bank-appraised market value less the outstanding mortgage). They can only be used for one's principal place of residence, and the property taxes, property insurance, and condition of the house need to be maintained. The cap on the appraised value of the home eligible for a reverse mortgage is currently $625,500. And the financing institution will take over your existing mortgage and bundle this with the funds supplied through the reverse mortgage at their interest rates. A quick reference for determining the potential size of the loan for a reverse mortgage can be found at www.mtgprofessor.com.

The money is basically a loan on the property. The income is not considered taxable income and will not impact your Social Security income. Money can be received in a monthly payment, in a lump sum, a credit line to use when needed, or a combination of all three. As the funds are used, the cumulative debt of the house increases in addition to the fees and interests due on the loan. When the house is sold, the total debt is then owed to the lending institution. If there is a surplus, the balance goes to yourself or your heirs. If there is a loss, then the gap may be paid by you or absorbed by the institution. In the case when the financial institution assumes the loss, nothing would go to your heirs, and the insurance that is bundled with the loan (and which you are accruing the fees annually) covers this loss to the institution. If you die or move out of the house, your estate or you generally have six months to sell the property and repay the loan. There are several features available for these programs, and one should be guided by a trusted financial advisor before deciding to use this option for funding one's lifestyle. If you are interested in exploring these programs be sure to review a study done by the Consumer Finance Protection Board (CFPB), which offers a clear assessment of the benefits and risks of these programs (https://www.consumerfinance.gov/data-research/research-reports/reverse-mortgages-report).

Another alternative source of income is to purchase an annuity. An annuity is an investment product purchased from an insurance company or financial institution. It is designed to be invested and grow and pay you an established flow of monthly payments starting on a set date. While there are many variations, they have some important advantages and disadvantages. For advantages, annuities have no contribution limits—unlike a 401(k) plan—and the investment returns on this income may not be taxable income. They can provide the security of a stable flow of income for the rest of your life. And, for some products, if there are remaining assets at your death, some of this will go to your beneficiary. For disadvantages, annuities are the most expensive investment instrument. There are many hidden fees and expenses that reduce your available cash. If you want to cancel the product, there are high surrender penalty fees. The investment returns are far less than standard investments, and if you die early, the insurance company can retain some or all of the asset balance. When the income is received, it is treated as ordinary income for tax purposes, and no capital gains tax treatment is possible. For some individuals, this will be an attractive investment vehicle, and for others, this will be an expensive way to receive a steady income flow that could be obtained through other mechanisms.

The primary task is to find the right balance between your financial resources and your lifestyle. It is critical to manage these resources well and guard against risks, shortfalls, major withdrawals, and fraud. As one moves from the stock market to bonds, the returns are likely lower, but the security will be higher. Moving from bonds to money market and secured investment accounts such as certificates of deposit (CDs) will lower the return but increase your income security. If you move to this investment philosophy, you will need to moderate the amount of any withdraw to reflect this lower rate of return. It may not produce the investment returns needed to meet your living expenses.

Illustration of a Financial Plan—Part 1: Doug and Kathy's Income

Doug (age sixty-five) and Kathy (age sixty-two) found each other as their kids were ending colleges and their lives were beginning to open up for them. They started their second marriage with great anticipation and concern. They were both fairly financially independent, although neither had sufficient resources to live comfortably for the remainder of their lives. Fortunately, they found each other, and through their sharing of assets and hearts, they found a balance between their financial resources and their desired lifestyle. They shaped their expectations to align with their resources so they could focus on what they enjoyed most: life together with fun, purpose, meaning, and adventure. We will examine how they examined their financial conditions and addressed the gaps they found. It will be easier to address these issues now than when the options may be more limited in the future.

Doug was turning sixty-five and was considering whether to retire. He realized he had been thinking about this for years, but now he had to make some decisions. Kathy was a few years younger, and she was deeply engaged in the decision process. They decided to work with a financial planner to test whether they could comfortably retire. They had saved throughout their lives through their employer-sponsored 401(k) plans and had made contributions to their savings when they had an especially large bonus for a given year. Because of this, they were able to develop a sizeable nest egg of investments. Most of these dollars were invested in a diverse range of mutual funds, approximately 70 percent in equities, and 30 percent in bonds or fixed-income investments. Indexed funds have been shown to mirror the overall stock market and have very low expenses. Consequently, the investment returns are based on a highly diverse portfolio, the returns are better than many actively managed funds (because the costs are lower), and the rate of return was good.

Their income sources were simple: a pension that Doug had from a previous long-term employer and income from both of their Social Security accounts. They used a financial advisor to determine their income projections and guide them on the proper investments to achieve the desired diversification of their assets and the desired annual return on investments. They also received an inheritance from the death of Doug's parents. Some of it was applied to the college expenses for their children, and the rest was put into their investment account. At this point, they have approximately $800,000 in their savings and investments. If they start their retirement now, their anticipated income will look like this:

Doug and Kathy's Income Projections		% of Total Income
Secured Income:		
Social Security: Doug starting at age 66	$ 17,695	
Pension: Doug	$ 16,000	
Social Security: Kathy starting at age 66	$ 12,250	
Total	$ 45,945	**55%**
Current total investments	$ 800,000	
Withdrawal from investments:		
Projected Investments when Doug is 65	$ 800,000	
4% withdrawal rate	$ 32,000	
5% withdrawal rate	$ 40,000	
CoRI withdrawal rate (20.29)	$ 39,428	
Average of 3 alternatives withdrawal rates	$ 37,143	**51%**
Total projected income	$ 83,088	% of Inc
Less provisions for state & Fed income taxes	$ 10,552	12.7%
Net after tax income	$ 72,536	

To calculate their income from investment sources, they decided to use a combination of percentages to determine the "safe" amount to withdraw from their invested assets. They used 4 percent, 5 percent, and the CoRI projections, and then they calculated an average of the three projection models. The $37,143 is 4.6 percent of the investment assets, which is well within the range of prudent withdrawals. They were not sure if this would be sufficient income, but they decided to test it out. If there was a gap, they were open to making changes to when they would stop working. Fortunately, both Doug and Kathy's employers were flexible about their continued working or taking retirement.

Determine How Much Will Be Needed (Expenses)

To determine how your income will be used, we start with understanding your needs and wants. Your needs may be those expenses you must pay in order to not be evicted or become homeless. Your wants may be those expenses that support the lifestyle you seek. The question is what spending level will be needed to meet the needs and wants that you defined in the chapter 4.

In addition, it is important to establish the timeframe you will use for your projections. Although current actuarial tables indicate that men will live to seventy-six and women till eighty-one, your plan should assume you will live to one hundred or longer. After all, you might just live that long. As you project your expenses, consider what you will be spending today will not be the same when you reach the Consolidation and Final stage. Your expenses will likely be significantly lower, except for perhaps medical or home-care expenses. In your projections, consider how your current expenses will change over the decades.

It is important to ascertain what you will likely need to live on financially for the next thirty or forty years. For example, what do you currently spend on housing, groceries, clothing, and taxes? What do you think you will be spending on travel, entertainment, and items that are more discretionary? Further, it will be important to consider whether you will need to support funding the education of grandchildren, help a son or daughter to buy a home or pay down college loans, support the expenses of graduate schools or business start-ups for your children, or find other ways to provide financial support to others in your family or circle of friends. How important is it to you to leave assets to your children? Should you plan on spending down your assets for as long as you can and leave whatever remains at the end to them and/or your favorite charity? When do you expect to have major expenses (buying a car, buying a vacation home, renovating your current home)? Finally, when you are projecting your living costs, consider what you expect the percentage increase in expenses will be due to inflation or other living requirements in housing, food, health care, entertainment, and general lifestyle.

A good place to start is to determine your current expenses. This task may take some reconstructive research and reviewing credit card statements, bank statements, and other receipts. It is important to know what these are before you make projections. Your financial planner is not likely to be able to produce these numbers for you. Then, once you have collected this information, put it in a form that you can understand, discuss with your spouse, talk about it, and decide what you think you will need for the next three to five years (each year's budget) as you plan the transition into your reinventing adulthood years.

A useful framework for examining your expenses is to categorize them into one of four types:

1) Fixed Expenses

These are expenses that you must pay on a monthly, quarterly, or annual basis. If you don't, there will be significant problems. Examples of these expenses are mortgage, taxes (local, state, and federal income-related and property taxes), premiums for insurance policies (life, auto, home, health, etc.), utilities (heat, air-conditioning, electricity, water, garbage recycling and removal, cable/internet, etc.) and medical expenses (prescriptions, medical copays, deductibles, etc.). This may also include assistance to a child with special needs. While you may be able to modify these expenses, they are the core ones that you must continue to pay.

2) Semifixed Expenses

These are expenses that are necessary but may vary based on usage or activities. Examples of these expenses are groceries, home maintenance, auto expenses (gas, repairs, etc.), family birthday gifts, Christmas or other holiday gifts, and health club dues or memberships. You will continue to have these expenses, but you may be able to adjust them to some degree if needed.

3) Variable Expenses

These are expenses that can be stopped if needed with minimum disruptions. You spend these because you want to and do these things if you have the income. Examples of these expenses are travel, entertainment, dinners out, contributions to charities, clothing, purchases for the home, and other items purchased or services acquired that bring entertainment and enjoyment to your life. Some of these may be regarded as semifixed because they provide joy and satisfaction you want and need in this stage of life.

4) Special Events

In every life, there may be pending major events, such as a wedding, or assistance needed for special schooling for grandchildren. One may be considering purchasing a new car or a vacation home—both of which may have a major but short-term impact on the family's financial conditions. There may be a down payment and then an increase in fixed expenses due to the increased debt of the major purchase.

By categorizing your historical expenses into these areas, you can see how fixed or flexible your expenses are. You can discuss and determine what expenses are really important versus nice to have. The discussion and clarity are perhaps more important than the numbers themselves. You can determine what level of income is needed to support your desired lifestyle. It is important to understand what you do now and then examine what will change as you progress through this Reinventing stage of adulthood. Some will increase, others will decrease, and much will remain unchanged.

You should forecast these expenses out over the next ten, twenty, or thirty years or for as long as you want to plan your financial requirements.

A spreadsheet or a retirement calculator may be helpful for this task. There are many calculators for putting your annual budget together on the internet—or you can use a spreadsheet of your own design. Your financial advisor may have tools to help you organize your expenses as well as project how they will likely increase over time. Realize that at some point, your expenses will decrease for the "go-slow" (Consolidation) stage or "no-go" (Final) stage, but health care expenses are likely to increase at this time. For example, your actual living expenses may decrease by 20 percent or 30 percent as you transition to these next stages of life, but in-home or nursing care may increase expenses by several thousand dollars per month. This is based on a mix of fixed, semifixed, and variable expenses. With this information, you can now examine whether what you have saved and accumulated sufficient wealth to cover these costs.

In addition to potential increases or decreases in one's planned or unplanned expenses, one's forecast should consider inflation. In brief, inflation is the rate (expressed as a percentage) that the costs for goods and services increase over a time period (deflation is the same only for a decrease in costs). This data is often expressed as the consumer price index (CPI), GNP deflator index, or the cost-of-living index. The cost-of-living factor does not usually impact every individual in the same way. How many times do you buy a new house, a new car, or new furniture? The expenses that are most susceptible to inflationary factors that impact everyday living include groceries, transportation, clothing, dining out, health care, and utilities. Since these are likely to be a major portion of your living expenses, projecting future expenses in relation to potential inflation will give you more clarity about what your actual expenses may likely be.

The average annual rate of inflation from 1913 to 2016 has been 3.22 percent, and it has been approximately 2.5 percent for the past twenty years. Therefore, in planning for the income needed to meet one's living expense budget, one should anticipate an annual increase in your expenses to be between 2.5 percent and 3 percent. Again, consult your financial advisor to determine this anticipated increase in your expenses.

Illustration of a Financial Plan—Part 2:
Doug and Kathy's Expenses

Let us look at what Doug and Kathy found when they examined their expenses. Their kids are out of the house, and this newly married couple is entering the Reinventing Stage of life. To address the question of their financial reality, they started with understanding their current (and historical) expenses. They then developed a model annual budget for this stage of their life and what they planned to do with their time. This gave them clarity about the financial resources needed to support their desired lifestyle. If they do not have enough income, then they will need to remain working, adjust their expenses, or plan to draw down more of their investments. This decision is important because they do not want to become a burden on their children because they overspent their income during this stage of life. Both Doug and Kathy felt very strongly about this life principle. Knowing this, with all the assumptions clear and known, will help them determine what actions are needed now.

This is what they developed for their model reinvention-stage budget based on examining their current expenses. They felt this was conservative but comfortable. Their model budget is shown below:

Doug and Kathy's Annual Budget			% of Total Expenses
Fixed Expenses:			
Mortgage	$	14,000	14%
Utilities: heat, electricity, water	$	7,000	7%
Taxes: Auto excise, Property	$	9,000	9%
Medical expenses and prescriptions	$	6,000	6%
Insurance - Life, health, home, auto	$	10,000	10%
Total Fixed Expenses:	*$*	*46,000*	**46%**
Semi-Fixed Expenses:			
Groceries	$	7,200	7%
Supplies and home maintenance	$	4,000	4%
Auto expenses -- gas, service	$	7,800	8%
Health club membership	$	2,000	2%
Gifts, Birthdays and Christmas	$	6,000	6%
Total Semi-Fixed Expenses:	*$*	*27,000*	**27%**
Variable Expenses:			
Dinners and Entertainment	$	7,000	7%
Contributions to church and charities	$	3,000	3%
Travel	$	5,000	5%
Doug's general expenses	$	4,000	4%
Kathy's general expenses	$	5,000	5%
Other/unplanned expenses	$	3,000	3%
Total Variable Expenses:	*$*	*27,000*	**27%**
Total Planned Expenses (Budget)	$	100,000	**100%**

When they excluded what they had spent on their children and contributions to their savings, they found their expenses would be approximately $100,000 per year. This was 85 percent of their current expenses during their full-time working careers. While some expenses move up and down depending on both controllable and uncontrollable expenses, Doug and Kathy felt confident that they could live a comfortable life on this amount of money.

This budget development process enabled them to have several important discussions about how they wanted to live their lives going forward. They looked at what would likely change about their current lifestyle and the likely impact on their expense projections:

- Will they be doing more travel? Should this budget be higher? For how many years?
- Will the costs they currently spend on health care increase or decrease as they move from an employer's insurance plan to Medicare or other similar plans?
- When will their mortgage be paid off? Do they want to downsize and use the equity that has been built into their current house to buy a smaller home or condo?
- They have a small term life insurance policy ($100,000 death benefit). Should they cancel it or keep it for income protection for the living spouse?
- They want to buy a car and second home or condo in a vacation area of their dreams. Can they afford this? If not now, when, if ever?
- Do they anticipate needing to pay for any of the educational or college expenses of their grandchildren? When would they anticipate this happening—and how much will they likely need to support their children's costs?
- If their living expenses are too high, should they consider moving to a lower-cost state? If so, where, when, and what would be the full impact of this move?
- Do they anticipate needing to support the expenses of Kathy's mother (her father died several years ago, and Doug's parents are deceased)? And what sort of inheritance may they anticipate with Kathy's mother's passing?

Once the model budget is determined, it is often important to examine and anticipate what may make a major impact on one's planned expenses. These may be planned, anticipated, or surprises. Doug and Kathy have these questions, and you may have similar ones. The importance of discussing the analysis and findings with your significant other/spouse cannot be overemphasized.

If this model budget holds well for supporting your lifestyle, the inflation growth in expenses will need to be covered by increases in your retirement income. Even though you can't predict the future, this budget exercise will give you a reference point on which to judge how well you are living within your means. It should be part of your Master Plan. This is an important factor in determining whether changes are needed now—when you are most capable of making them.

How the Numbers Add Up

The task now turns to putting these two pieces together—your projected income and your anticipated expenses:

- How well does your current projected income cover your planned expenses?
- How much income will you need over what time period to live the life that you imagined?
- What can you do to provide peace of mind, protection from risk, with the desired growth and use of your assets?

The answers to these questions should enable you to determine the level of comfort, risk, or change needed to secure the desired future. The conclusions may require one to either "raise the bridge" (increase income) or "lower the water" (reduce expenses) when it comes to the providing for enough income to live the life you want and deserve. This means you may need to increase the sources of income or reduce the anticipated expenses. A helpful framework for determining the level of change needed is to view the results on the following scale:

Level 1: Significant Deficit

This means you have a major problem. Your expenses are too high for the income that you anticipate (expenses exceed your projected income by at least 20 percent). While it may not be impacting you while you are still earning income, it will when this income stops. This will most likely require you to live a more modest life, a simpler life, a more personally or family-focused life. This may mean you will need to continue working and earning income for the foreseeable future. This does not mean you cannot have adventures and joy, but you must find ways to increase your income or reduce the costs associated with your lifestyle. Look for where you can increase your earned income for a longer time period and adjust your life to find joy and pleasure in these activities. Look for where you can reduce your expenses because it may be that some of the expenses are no longer important to you or your family. Getting to a place where you can be confident, comfortable, and secure will generate significant peace of mind and fulfilment in the next stage of your life. You are the most challenged, but you can find solutions to these challenges. Seriously simplify your life, be careful, and appreciate what you have.

Level 2: Moderate Deficit

This means that your expenses exceed your projected income by 10 or 20 percent. While drastic changes may not be necessary, this condition is not sustainable. Examine what expenses can be reduced now so that your future expenses can realize more balance in your anticipated income. And examine what you can do to continue earning some of your previous income for as long as possible. This is an important principle. Changes now are usually easier and will have a profound, positive impact on your life, but the changes need to be identified and implemented. You may consider a strategy that gradually spends down your investments. If this is pursued, remember that your investment income will drop as you spend your assets on living expenses and cause you to increase your withdrawal rates as you get older. You will need adequate reserves in case you live longer than expected. It is important to you and your family to prevent a crisis from impacting your life at a time when you will be least able to address it. Take action now—while you can.

Level 3: Relative Balance

This means that your income and expense are relatively in balance. This means your income or expenses are within 5–10 percent of the other. If expenses are slightly higher than projected income, you may need to make some small but important changes to your activities or make certain adjustments regarding your sources of income. You may be able to live off your assets or spend down your assets, leaving what remains to your children, family, or charities. All in all, things are in balance, but your financial condition will need to be carefully and frequently monitored. Congratulations, and remember to monitor, adapt, and enjoy.

Level 4: Moderate Surplus

This means that your projected income is higher than anticipated expenses by perhaps 10–20 percent. While it appears that you can afford your plans, care must be taken to monitor and ensure these assets and income—and your expenses—remain in positive territory. Periodic adjustments may be needed, but you can pursue the activities you want. Enjoy and appreciate what you have been given and have created.

Level 5: Significant Surplus

This means that your projected income exceeds your anticipated expenses by 20–30 percent or more. You do not anticipate the need to worry about whether or not you will be able to afford the lifestyle you seek. Your questions should be about legacy, family trusts, and multigenerational estate planning. You should periodically monitor both income and expenses, but the reality is you should have little real concern unless there is a major event that changes these conditions. Enjoy life. You are one of the fortunate ones.

Illustration of a Financial Plan—Part 3: Doug and Kathy Put It All Together

Doug and Kathy examined their projected expenses, considering many wants and ideas for the future. They realized that their secured income (from Social Security and his pension) plus the 4.6 percent withdrawal from assets would not cover their expenses. The gap was 29 percent (projected after tax income of $72,536 and expenses of $100,000—a gap of $27,464 a year). While this put them in level 1 (significant deficit) described above, there are several things they can do to improve the situation. There are many elements in the life plan that can impact this financial gap, and they should examine how the shortfall can be minimized through their actions. They are not feeling this now because they are both working and earning income. When this income stops, then they will have serious reasons to worry.

They focused on the income side. First, they realized if they held off using any of their investment income, and it continued to grow at 6 percent, then this would increase their assets from $800,000 to $1,134,815 (or an increase of $334,815) in five years. This would produce an additional $15,545 annual income using the same 4.6 percent withdrawal rate. Second, by not taking their Social Security until they were both seventy, they could increase their annual income by more than $14,000. Third, they could add another $100,000 to their investment assets by putting Doug's pension income ($80,000 over five years) into investments.

Then, they looked at their expenses and started identifying areas where they could change their planned expense budget to be closer within their means. They felt they could reduce their expenses by $4,000 a year and gain another $20,000 when they were seventy and begin their retirement fully. This would reduce the gap to $13,500. They were able to reduce about $7,500 from their expenses. When they used a 2.5 percent inflation factor to estimate their expenses when Doug was seventy, the new expense budget was $105,000. This resulted in a deep sigh of relief. This approximately $5,000 a year deficit was well within their ability to manage given the anticipated inheritance from her mother's estate and the realization that when they were in their eighties and nineties (the Consolidation stage), their expenses would likely be reduced by 20–30 percent or more if they didn't need in-home special care. The chart below shows what they would achieve by implementing these simple measures.

Doug and Kathy's Revised Financial Projections		% of Total
Secured Income:		
Social Security: Doug starting at age 70	$ 26,000	
Pension: Doug	$ 16,000	
Social Security: Kathy starting at age 70	$ 18,000	
Total	**$ 60,000**	**51%**
Withdrawal from investments:		
Projected Investments when Doug is 70	**$ 1,234,815**	
4% withdrawal rate	$ 49,393	
5% withdrawal rate	$ 61,741	
CoRI withdrawal rate (20.29)	$ 60,858	
Average of 3 alternatives withdrawal rates	**$ 57,331**	**49%**
Total projected income	$ 117,331	% of Inc
Less provisions for state & Fed income taxes	$ 17,717	15.1%
Net after tax income	**$ 99,614**	
Revised annual expense projections	**$ 105,000**	
Gap: Net surplus or (Net loss)	**$ (5,386)**	
As a percent of their expenses	-5%	

They examined their planned spending and a conservative approach to their investment projections and decided that this model would work for them. By implementing this plan, they saw themselves in level 3 (balanced) as described above; their assets would likely cover their anticipated expenses, although it would not leave much for their children if they lived to this age. If they needed the additional capital and were still in their house (wouldn't that be wonderful?), they could consider using a home-equity credit line or other assets available at that time. This then assured them that they would have adequate reserve to carry them if their actual expenses exceeded the budget. They would need to monitor their investment returns and spending as they live their lives together; they were ready to do this because their life together was important. They knew that their financial condition would limit some of their plans, and they accepted this challenge because they knew the facts on which this was based.

The Importance of a Financial Plan

Determining whether you will have the money you need requires careful and thorough examination of how you live and how you anticipate the future. It is important to examine the income potential from your assets in context with the expenses you anticipate. For many, the current conditions are the result of many past decisions (some good and some not so wise). They may reflect a little good luck or bad fortune. Regardless of the sources, knowing is better than avoiding—even if the assumptions or findings are difficult to hear. The primary purpose of this analysis is to provide support for the plans and desires you have for this next stage of your life. Then, once the financial plan is set, go and focus your time, energy, and passions on the things you do and want to do. In many domains of life, it is all about balance and remaining focused on the elements that give you purpose, meaning, and joy. It is just that simple and that important.

Chapter 6

Who Do You Want to Live With?

*If you live to be one hundred, I hope I live to be one hundred
minus one day, so I never have to live without you.*
—**Winnie the Pooh**

We are social creatures. Much of our sense of self comes from the relationships we have with other people. While the title of this chapter implies a single relationship, all forms of relationships will be changing as we enter this Reinventing adulthood stage of life. You may be considering numerous changes for yourself in this stage, and it is important to examine the impact they will have on your relationships—with your spouse/significant other, previous coworkers and colleagues, friends, children, and communities. In the previous chapters, we examined what you want to do with your time and your financial resources. In subsequent chapters, we're going to examine how to remain healthy and who you want to become. While each of these areas is interdependent, relationships often form the bond that tie many of these things together. An entire chapter is devoted to relationships because relationships have been shown to be a major factor in both longevity and quality of life. Since this is a time of significant change and transition, examining one's full spectrum of relationships is very important for paving the pathway to the desired life experience.

Relationships Matter

Relationships are at the core of many decisions and ways we treat ourselves and others. This includes both a primary relationship and people who live in close community with each other. The reasons that relationships have such a positive impact on one's life has to do with the number of interactions, the emotional nourishment, and the degree of support one receives in one's living arrangement. Loneliness, in turn, leads individuals to experience greater stress, anxiety, and more problems with simply daily living.

Numerous studies have shown that strong, positive relationships lead to better health. A study cited in the Harvard Women's Health Watch[29] of more than 309,000 people found that the lack of strong relationships appeared to increase the risk of premature death from all causes by 50 percent. The effect is similar to smoking up to fifteen cigarettes a day—and even greater for people who are obese or lacking in physical activity. Another study of 127,545 American adults found that men who were married were healthier than men who were divorced, widowed, or never married. The conclusion was that married men tend to live healthier lives than unmarried men, but this is not true for women. Women who have a core group of "sisters" (two or three very close friends) tended to do better than those living basically alone. The marriage did not have much influence on women in longevity unless it was an unhealthy one, and then the impact was negative.[30]

The reason health improves appears to be rooted in understanding stress and the impact of stress on human biology. Marital stress and conflicts produce elevated adrenaline, which in turn increases inflammation and blood pressure. The impact of stress is discussed more fully in chapter 7. Behavioral factors also contribute to the reduction of the longevity factor, especially in men. Men who are unmarried, divorced, or widowed simply don't eat as well or exercise

---

[29]   "The Health Benefits of Strong Relationships," *Harvard Women's Health Watch Newsletter*, published December 2010.

[30]   Charlotte A. Schoenborn, MPH, "Marital Status and Health: United States, 1999–2002," Center for Disease Control, Division of Health Interview Statistics, Number 351 + December 15, 2004.

sufficiently. They tend to smoke, drink excessively, and engage in other risky behaviors. In contrast, women—both single and in a relationship—are more likely to get regular checkups and do more preventative health practices, especially when they are in close relationships with "sisters." This is also true for senior citizens who live with a spouse rather than living alone. Many women create and retain close connections with their children. These relationships transform from parent-child to two (or more) people who share a core, common connection that is deeper than found among friends. Betsy values her short and long-term friends and says, "I am blessed."

Marital unhappiness and stress have been linked to increases in cardiac risk factors and hypertension for both women and men. Over time, marital stress is associated with thickening of the heart's primary pumping chamber, but stress from the job did not have a similar effect on the heart. The study found that even after serious problems developed, a supportive marriage is correlated with improved survival rates. In another study cited in Harvard Women's Health Watch, women who were in highly satisfying marriages or marital-type relationships had a lower risk of cardiovascular disease.

The second major killer as we grow older is cancer. While there is little evidence that married life or relationships have any connection to contracting the disease, studies have shown that strong, positive relationships help improve the outcomes. In a study of 27,779 cancer patients, scientists found that unmarried individuals were more likely to have advanced disease at the time of the first diagnosis than married persons. Unmarried people were less likely to seek out a diagnosis when a problem first emerges or receive regular treatments than married people. Individuals who had intact marriages when the cancer was diagnosed had a better survival rate than patients who were separated or divorced at the time of the diagnosis.[31]

Finally, Jim Coan at the University of Virginia has conducted a number of studies between friendships and health and believes that friends enable you to turn off stress hormones, lower blood pressure,

---

[31]   Goodwin JS, Hunt WC, Key CR, Samet JM. "The Effect of Marital Status on Stage, Treatment, and Survival of Cancer Patients," *JAMA*. 1987;258(21):3125–3130.

reduce inflammation, and boost one's immune system. Studies also found that active people have less memory loss than those who were less engaged.[32]

The conclusion is that close personal relationships matter, and they tend to impact lives in several ways. First, people tend to lead healthier lifestyles when they are in a primary relationship or have a core group of close friends. Health in women tends to be affected less by their primary relationships perhaps because women are often used to seeing a doctor when they face physical difficulties. Second, strong positive relationships have been shown to decrease stress and provide important nurturing to strengthen the individual's ability to fight disease. If women have a core group of friends, they often support each other when addressing an illness; this is not as often true with men and their non-spouse relationships. Finally, when one does become sick, the outcomes are better for people who are in primary relationships. Not only do they tend to seek regular checkups, they address the disease earlier than those who live independently. This speaks to the importance of having a close circle of friends (and/or family members) who know you, look out for you, and encourage you to take care of yourself.

How Strong Relationships Are Created

Poets, songwriters, and mystics have much to say about relationships and what makes them sincere and meaningful. I will not attempt to define what makes an enriching relationship, but I will share some important considerations about relationships as we enter this stage of life. The following factors tend to create, strengthen, and reinforce strong relationships:

---

[32] Coan, James A., Hillary S. Schaefer, Richard J. Davidson, "Lending a Hand: Social Regulation of the Neural Response to Threat," *Psychological Science*, December 1, 2006.

1) Shared Experiences

A relationship is developed through shared experiences and a history one has with the other person. In a family, you create a history of experiences, traditions, and ways of being. In friendships, it is often time and activities you spend together that deepen the relationships. You talk about opinions and share life-shaping stories, personal feelings, and struggles. Deep relationships can take a long time to build. Depending on the openness one has to the emotions and the degree to which one feels the other person truly listens, understands, and cares, the relationship can become truly significant. Some of these experiences are created by external events, and some are created by talking, sharing, and experiencing the heart of the other person.

Where were you on September 11, 2001? Who were you with? Do you feel a special bond with them? Are there other experiences you have had that have created a relationship with others? What about work experiences, a major project, or the launch of a new business, product, or project? If you were in the military, Peace Corps, or other personally challenging situation, you've probably created a bond with the people where you shared commons experiences that were intense, deep and important.

There are many things that create and strengthen relationships. You just need to be open to the experience and the emotions that were shared between you and the other person or people. Because shared experiences are critical to an enduring relationship, it takes time to develop them. Most of us have these experiences and the relationships from which they come.

2) A History of Expectations and Experiences

By expectations, I mean that you enter or live in a relationship (i.e., a new friend, the renewal of an old friendship, a work colleague) with certain expectations about what you want (or need) from them. The more your expectations are aligned the other person's actions, the greater the chances for a successful relationship. By experiences, I mean what you feel over time is often highly influenced by the other person and your interpretations. You control the impact of the other person, and what they do also matters; both receive equal credit for the conditions of the relationship. Relationships are complicated and necessary.

At times, the person's actions run counter to what you want or need. This may cause stress, distrust, or hurt feelings; sometimes these are unintended, and other times, they are intended. The experience you had just simply did not meet your expectations. At other times, the person provides something that was unexpected and wonderful. You feel the person gets you, understands you at a deeper level, and gives you something special.

These are normal dynamics in all relationships. Compromise and adjusting expectations to the other person's characteristics are also critical ingredients for a successful relationship. If these expectations are not fulfilled, then you need to determine how important they are in relation to the other value you receive from this relationship. We can't always get what we need from certain individuals, which is often why we need to have more than one person in our lives. This is why some relationships endure and others dissolve.

3) Trust, Understanding, and Appreciation

These factors become the bonds of the relationship. Trust that the person will be there for you. Understand that they know your needs. Appreciate what they provide for you. Do they appreciate what you provide for them? The levels that these attributes are experienced often define the depth of a relationship. All relationships are complex and have moments when these attributes are challenged. It is often important to see what happens when these bonds are tested. This is perhaps more important than having the belief or expectation that they won't be tested. The response to problems is often more important than the existence of problems. The question becomes whether the desired experiences outweigh other experiences to retain a proper balance with your needs and their actions—and your actions compared to their needs.

While most of this balance between the histories of experiences, meeting one's expectations or needs—and having a strong sense of trust—creates a relationship that is filled with joy and caring. While a deep level of this is more characteristic of one's primary relationship, it may also relate to one's coworkers, friends, neighbors, fellow club members, and relatives.

Changing the Nature of Your Relationships

It is important at this time to examine the implications of your current and future journey on the relationships that you have with others. Many of them may change in fundamental ways—some growing closer and others becoming more distant. This is natural and expected. After all, you may be leaving a workplace where you had many friends and colleagues. You may become more involved in new organizations, clubs, or community settings where new relationships will form. The time you spend at home may change the relationship you have with your spouse or significant partner. New agreements about home responsibilities may emerge and need to be renegotiated with changes in both expectations and behaviors. All of these factors impact the mosaic in the pattern of relationships.

Within this context of change, there are six different pathways one may take when it comes to your primary relationship. This is important because depending on the actions you take, you may need to change the community of relationships in which you live. This range of alternatives may take time to develop since each can have profound implications on what you do with your time, where you decide to live, and how you are going to live. They may also impact your financial conditions. While these pathways are about one's primary relationship, they impact all important relationships you have. Let's examine the pathways as you enter this next stage of life.

1) Keep On Keeping On

For this pathway, you decide for yourself or with your significant other (and others) that things are going well in the relationship, and the relationship will easily (and perhaps joyfully) adjust to the changes taking place in both of your lives. In other words, you both view this as the time you want to pursue areas of mutual interest. This could be adventure travel, improving one's golf, tennis, running, cycling, or going to museums or movies during the week. You both easily adapt to the changes being planned or underway. Both the expectations change, and each makes needed adjustments to behaviors so that the relationship continues as it has in the past. It may in fact become richer. No significant change is needed, and what is not fulfilled does not outweigh the value of the relationship. In other words, those things that you have defined as not meeting your expectations are not as important as those things that do meet your expectations and fulfill your core needs. No relationship fulfills the full range of one's needs, but the decision is both a rational and emotional. The benefits outweigh the limitations. The relationship truly adds value to your life and your significant other's life. You contribute to the betterment of this person's life.

2) Deepening Your Relationship: Renewing Your Vows

For this pathway, you decide together that the relationship should remain primary and desire to mark this decision through a ceremony. For many couples, they decide to have a second wedding ceremony to renew their vows and commitments to each other. These are times for the family to celebrate the relationship—and often have a wonderful party. This may be an intimate or an extravagant affair. The key point of this pathway is that you and your significant other make a renewed commitment to each other, witnessed by the friends and family who support you. This can be a milestone experience that reminds each person of the importance and value received from the other person and the relationship. Richard and Kate and Toby and David both created ceremonies where they renewed their vows. They were surrounded by children, family, and friends, and they all saw it as a major renewing event in their lives.

3) Separate but Equal

For this pathway, you decide to live separate lives but remain married or connected in some significant manner. Some responsibilities and costs continue to be shared, and others will be fulfilled independently. For example, Phillip and Susan decided to live separately but not get divorced. This was a mutual decision. They wanted to continue being active in the lives of their children and other activities that they shared—but live in separate houses. Fortunately, they could afford this duplication of the costs, and they did not go through the pain and expense of a divorce. They could pursue relationships with other people, but these would be limited. If the other person were to find a new significant other, then they would pursue a formal separation and/or divorce. But until then, they found that living separately was less stressful than living together, and this had many desired benefits.

4) Divorce and Move On

This pathway would terminate the formal relationship, but depending on the terms, a different level of friendship could be maintained. This involves renegotiating the expectations of a new relationship with one's former spouse. While the overall divorce rate in the US and other developed countries has stabilized, the divorce rate for people over sixty is growing dramatically. It is still a small percentage of the population, but the divorce rate for this age group has grown dramatically. In a study conducted by Bowling Green State University based on an analysis of US Census, divorce rates for people sixty-five and older has more than tripled, from two per thousand in 1990 to six per thousand in 2012. This is the fastest-growing divorce rate of any group.[33] If you choose this path, you are not alone. This experience is filled with sadness and disappointment—as well as new beginnings and hope for a better life in the future. It is often important to realize that if certain needs are core to your identity and health are not being met in this relationship, it is better

---

[33]   Susan Brown and I-Fen Lin, "The Gray Divorce Revolution," National Center for Family and Marriage Research at Bowling Green State University paper, 2009.

for both to move on and perhaps form a different kind of relationship. The benefits need to outweigh the costs.

5) New Connections or New Marriages

Following the ending of a relationship, many people seek another primary relationship. Starting a new relationship at this stage of life is, at best, awkward. It is likely to have been many years since you went out on a date. The number of websites that cater to singles over fifty has also grown dramatically to meet the demand for people seeking people with whom they can establish a new relationship. What are you looking for in this next relationship? How do you assess the person you are getting to know? What level of flexibility do you need to have—and the other person needs to give—in order for the relationship to blossom? Is this person just a friend, play companion, or a friend with benefits? When do you have sex? What will the children think? What will your friends think when you bring this person to a party or over for dinner? Is this person financially secure so you won't need to cover their needs? Will you need to take care of this person's financial needs as well? Are you sufficiently open and flexible to developing a new relationship at this stage of life? These are just some of the questions that may race through your mind if you are seeking to develop a new primary relationship. In a study by Pew Research, people who remarried over the age of fifty-five grew from 42 percent in 1980 to 57 percent by 2013. Further, the interest in remarrying was higher among men than women. The Pew Research findings shows that 29 percent of divorced or widowed men were interested in remarrying—but only 15 percent of women were interested.[34]

6) Deciding to Remain Single

Often the greatest fear about deciding to remain single is that you will be alone. Who can you count on to be there for you? Who can take you

---

[34] Pew Research Center analysis of 2013 American Community Survey (1 percent IPUMS).

to the doctor or hospital? Who can you have dinner with? Who will ask you about your day? Who can you share a laugh with about a situation? Who will keep your head on straight as you struggle with a problem?

For others, there is a freedom and flexibility that is enjoyed far beyond what they anticipated when first separated from a long-term relationship. Both emotional conditions are true. You enjoy the quietness that only comes from living alone. You have the flexibility to be with others or not, you can lead your life without compromise, and you can have relationships that come and go—with no particular demands or expectations. The challenge is to find the friendships and a community that will provide the right level of affiliation, connections, security, companionship, and intimacy you want as you continue with life.

The greatest fear is being alone at a time when your health is challenged or starts fading. To address this fear, the individual must take the initiative to develop a community that meets ongoing as well as future needs. It appears that the key to living successfully on one's own is when you create and appreciate a core group of "sisters" or "brothers" who may actually be closer to you than your actual family is. They provide the community that looks out for you, care for and about you, and you do the same for them. Or, your family becomes the support group you need. This connection, it appears from experience and the research cited in this chapter, is an essential element to a long and meaningful life.

7) When a Spouse Dies

Sometimes bad and sad things happen to good people. While, in most cases, the woman is left the widow, men experience this too. Working through the emotional trauma and process of healing when one loses a spouse, often the best friend, is very difficult and beyond the scope of this book. For those who have gone through this experience, they often find it takes years before a real relationship can be considered. For Bill, Mary, and Biff, all of whom lost their loving spouses, the transition to a new life has taken years, but it did come. At the early stages of this loss, they each felt alone, overwhelmed by the responsibility, and deeply sad, sensitive, and vulnerable.

Life following the death of one's spouse is full of grief and loneliness and often activities are manufactured to keep one busy and distracted from the deep, emotional sadness one is experiencing. Some persons may want to jump back into a relationship quickly, but research has shown this is not a wise thing to do. Time does heal, but it may take several years—and the loss never goes away. Let your emotional self just go through its healing process, and you will come out on the other side a different—but healthier—person. If this has been your experience, there are many books, resources, and counselors to help you with this experience. You are not alone. The ultimate goal is to reframe your life's path and seek new, enriching areas for growth and meaning. The loss can never be replaced, but your life can continue to be fulfilling and important. That is probably what your lost partner would have wanted. You will be okay in time—just give yourself this time.

Biff does one thing that has become especially important since his wife died several years ago. He gets up early each day, makes the bed, keeps his apartment clean and organized, and goes out for some exercise. He thanks the discipline he learned while serving in the military. At times, he knows he could let this go, but he doesn't allow himself to do this. He wants the discipline of a regular life. He is stronger and determined to live a considerate, thoughtful life. He has not lost his sense of humor and knows the importance of laughing. "Without the ability to laugh and laugh at oneself, life would be pretty boring." While he misses his best friend greatly, he knows that he can create a life that is full of friends, family, and experiences if he takes care of himself. He is giving himself permission to enter into a new relationship. After several years, Bill did the same thing. Time does have a way of healing.

Since rebuilding her life after her husband died about eight years ago, Mary has become an active cyclist, hiker, skier, and adventure seeker. While she has a lot of great girlfriends and strong relationships with her children and grandchildren, she would like to find a guy, build a relationship, and grow old together. The trouble is that she is seventy, and most men want younger women. Men who would find her "younger" just can't keep up with this dynamic person. This is an experience that women in this next stage frequently encounter.

Types of Relationships

We can now understand why relationships are important for everyone. As we examine relationships, we realize that there are a broad range of them. Research has shown that on average, humans can maintain approximately 150 people in their network of relationships. There is obviously a range of depth in these relationships. There is usually an inner core of people that usually includes about three to five people. Then, the next layer includes about fifteen people. Then, in the third layer, we can usually maintain about fifty people. The layers expand the number of people but the lower the level of intimacy. This is called Dunbar's number.[35]

Relationships require investments in time, emotion, and sharing of oneself. They require taking time to listen and express caring about what the other person is experiencing. The closer the person is to you, the more the relationship deepens—and you both benefit from it. You care more, and what the other person does matters. And there are those with whom you have limited contact or a relationship that is defined by an area of interest that you share. Your expectations or needs and wants are fulfilled through a series of relationships.

One way that people keep relationships active is by constantly updating each other on what's happening in their lives. This means a call or time to get together at least once per week for the inner core and at least once or several times a month for the next layer. Frequent communication and sharing are the investments that create the relationships that produce the desired health and life benefits. Social media tools have had a major impact on how people remain informed about and communicate with friends, especially those who live far away.

Suzanne has been able to maintain a core group of friends that goes back to their childhoods. They get together as friends (without husbands or children) annually, and the conversations often pick up where they left off. They share deep stories, feelings, and experiences with their "sisters" and look forward to the next time. While Suzanne lives several thousands of miles from her core group, they are still very important to

---

[35]   Pádraig MacCarron, Kimmo Kaski, Robin Dunbar, *Calling Dunbar's Numbers*, Cornell University Library, August 2016.

her. She wishes she could have shared more of their times when they were in their thirties, forties, and fifties, but the bonds are still there.

Eric and Laurie and four other couples inadvertently became an unusual and important group. They started when sitting at the same table at a charitable auction, they spontaneously decided to bid together on a weekend at a beautiful cabin on a lake in the mountains of New England. What started out as a single event turned into an annual pilgrimage for the group. They have also traveled together to Italy and elsewhere, and they often meet every couple of months to check in. Each person is given time to share what they are doing, feeling, or worried about and describe their joys and concerns. Everyone is there to listen, support, and cherish this very special kinship. For some, this group has become closer than their own siblings, and are their *intentional family.*

These people hold and reinforce a range of relationships. Below are descriptions of five levels of relationships. Each progresses out from the center through a series of concentric circles, each one larger but farther from the core. Like the orbit of planets, or expanding sound waves, each level has certain characteristics. These levels define the different types of relationships you will likely have with people in your life. While this may sound rather simple, the important task is to map your relationships and then reflect on this picture.

As you begin to see this social system, this community, this range of friendship around you, you can identify where the important ones are and where the gaps are. As your life and the relationships that used to be part of your everyday life change, where do you feel a hole or an absence? This is the purpose and importance of mapping your range of relationships—so you can understand what exists today and what you would like to change for the future. A father may realize he has let the connections with his children to grow distant; the woman may realize the importance of her group of sisters; a retired professional may see the value she or he received from the work team and wants to create a new team with which to share new challenges. A man may realize that only his wife is in the core circle, and he needs to create some brothers to enrich his world. Then you can hopefully make those adjustments needed to build a community of relationships that helps bring greater meaning and quality to your life.

1) Core/Life Partners

These are the two to three people that you talk with frequently and share most of what is going on in your life. You have a strong level of intimacy with them and they are your best friends forever. This may include your spouse and two to three core friends. You see each other regularly and can talk about most anything from the trivial to the deeply personal. You know them, and they know you, at levels known by few others. You reach out to them when you are most troubled; they may reach out to you for the same. You also have many shared experiences, values, and perspectives, discuss deep personal things from time to time, and look out for each other in many ways. They are like your spouse, brothers, and sisters; they are your life partners.

2) Family or Family-Like

These are people who either are actual members of your family or clearly feel that way. They may be your brothers and sisters (if they are not in the "core group."). Not all family relationships are as strong as the core group, but there is always a close connection to these people. Your actual family members may not necessarily be in this level. These people are important to you; you see them as your family. Your interactions may be monthly or tied to certain celebrations or holidays. There is clearly a shared history, but you likely share many of each other's values. The ties that keep you together are strong and important. When you don't see each other for a long time, and then meet again, it feels like the conversation picks up where you left off.

3) Close Friends

These are people who you regard as close friends. You have dinners together, go to the movies or events together, and do other social activities. You discuss life, times, and other things that are important to life. You are interested in things they do as much as they are interested in what you do. You are happy to see them and look forward to getting together. They are always on your invite list when you have a party or social event. These are people you want around you for milestone birthdays and other major celebrations of life. They are your good friends, but they are not quite family.

4) Your Community

These are people where you have some important things in common. This may be a church, a social club, or an activity. These are people who you share something with, but they do not know you that well. They know you and respect you, but they are not people you need to stay in touch with on a regular basis. They are kindred souls. They may be coworkers or individuals you used to work with, and you stay in touch periodically. You enjoy seeing them, and there may be individuals you want to get to know better, and they are good part of your community. Further, there may be many communities to which you belong. There may be a community who shares activities you enjoy, a religious faith community, sporting friends, or a neighborhood. You may have a series of circles or communities to which you belong that will either increase, decrease, or continue as you move into this next stage of life. A community is an important infrastructure for one's social existence. Consequently, you may have several communities in which you feel a part. There may be some overlap in the individuals, but there are specific areas of interests, activities, or experiences you have in common that form the basis for the relationship. Few people have just one community; most have a constellation of communities.

5) Your Network of Acquaintances

These are people you know, and they know you, at least by name and a few associations. They may be individuals who you have worked with or interacted with in a very limited manner. They are good people, but you don't really know much about them. There are a lot of these people in your network, and you value some of their connections. All in all, these are people who have limited influence on your life, and you are theirs. However, they are people you know and may at some occasion get to know them better. In short, this is your network of relationships.

These descriptions of the type of relationships help us understand where different people are within our spheres of influence. A sphere defines how much influence one has on your life and how much influence you have on them. It is important to understand these levels because they can shape the expectations you have for the relationships and require you to adjust behaviors in accordance with the level of relationship you have with them and they have with you. In the context of relationships and health, it is important to understand your circles of relationships, what changes are needed, and how to enrich them going forward.

Mapping Your Relationships

As discussed earlier, your life is changing, and the direction you are taking may be different than in your past. You may leave the workplace environment and the community of interests that you shared in some commercial endeavor. You may be looking to strengthen a core circle of friends because you realize the importance they have on your health and life and want to make changes in these relationships. Some relationships are going to grow more distant, and others will become deeper and more intimate.

As you develop your Master Plan throughout the reading of this book, do an exercise now that will identify who is in different levels of relationship with you. Take a piece of paper and draw a series of five concentric circles, each one larger than the one before it. Start with a small circle in the center of the page and expand the circles as you fill up the page (an example is shown below). Now, list the names of people (or groups) who are in each of these circles in relation to your level of relationships with them. Use the five levels defined earlier. List the specific names of most of the people, knowing that you do not need to include everyone you know. As you move farther out from the center, the names may be more representative of people or groups you know and relationships you have. Do this until you have considered all those who are important and interested in your life.

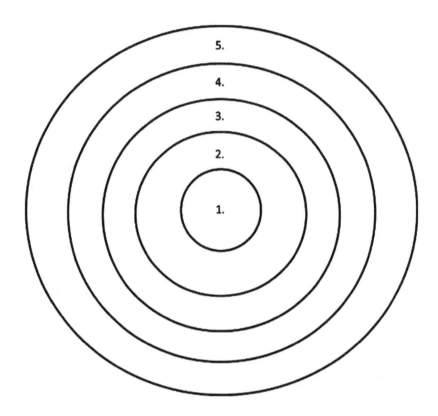

Once this task has been done, look at what you have developed. Ask yourself these questions:

- How do you feel about this? What does this make you think of or feel about the number and types of relationships you have?
- Do you feel comforted by the number and strength of these relationships? Do you feel aware of your separation from people who should play a more important role in your life?
- Do you sense a level of regret or appreciation for what you have laid out before you?
- Where do you feel at risk or vulnerable about your relationships?
- What would you like to change, if anything?

Relationships, and sustaining them, is hard and important. Without them, life becomes more problematic and increases the risk of finding more loneliness than community in this new stage of life. While there may be temporary changes, it is important to find those that make a difference in your life and determine if those people provide you with the experiences that you want to have with them. They simply provide the emotion connections that hold many of your parts together and on which your life may depend.

Chapter 7
How Do You Stay Healthy?

To me, good health is more than just exercise and diet. It's really
a point of view and a mental attitude you have about yourself.
—Albert Schweitzer

As we have discovered, our living longer has created this next
stage: Reinventing Adulthood. It is simply that people, especially
in the developed world, are living longer than in any other time
in human history. There are many factors creating this phenomenon,
and we will examine the most important research published so far (more
is coming every year) and learn what we can do to not only extend our
own lives but extend the quality of our lives.

Perhaps the most difficult uncertainties of this stage are the issues
people have with their health. Flexibility, endurance, and recovery
pose greater challenges as we live through this stage. As we enter the
Reinventing Adulthood stage, change may happen gradually, but there
are moments when you realize that you can't do what you used to do,
and this usually is because of your body's condition. Individuals often
deny that they are growing older, facing more limitations, or seeing
things differently. Experiencing this denial period is understandable as
long as it doesn't prevent you from taking certain actions. The question
is what to do about it. How do you stay healthy?

Current Research on Aging and Longevity

The baby boom generation continues to impact society. As this group enters this next stage, their interests and numbers are influencing research, development, and services in many areas of society. The research shows that approximately 25 percent of longevity is due to one's genetic makeup, and 75 percent is due to one's own behaviors and the environment.[36] This is important because if we use certain behaviors, we may be able to lengthen our own lives and strengthen the quality of those lives. This means that you have choices about how you live your life, and there are direct consequences (positive or negative) to the choices that you make.

When does old age start? A study by the Pew Research Institute found that 70 percent of Americans want to live to one hundred years old. However, the consensus across all ages is that "old age" begins at sixty-eight, according to Pew Research of 2,969 survey respondents. However, those who were 50–64 felt old age started at seventy-two; those over sixty-five saw old age starting at seventy-four. For individuals who were seventy-five or older, only 35 percent felt that they were old.[37] The conclusion is that you are old if you think you are.

How long can you expect to live? The National Institutes on Aging published research that most people born in 1900 did not live to fifty. Some of this was due to infant mortality. However, now the overall average life expectancy in the United States is 78.8[38]. The life expectancy for women is 81.2 years and for men is 76.4. Life expectancy has been steadily increasing. From 1840 to 2007, life expectancy has increased by about three months each year. Between 2010 and 2050, the number of people who are over 85 will increase by 351 percent—and people over 100 will increase 1,004 percent.[39] Two-thirds of the growth in life expectancy has developed in the latter parts of the twentieth century,

---

[36] Giuseppe, Pasarino, Francesco De Rango and Alberto Montesanto, "Human Longevity: Genetics or Lifestyle?," *Immun Ageing*, 2016, 13:12.

[37] "Growing Old in America: Expectations vs. Reality," Pew Research Center.

[38] 2014 Report by the Centers for Disease Control of the US Department of Health and Human Services.

[39] United Nations, World Populations Prospects: The 2010 Revision. October 2011.

and this growth continues to expand. Now more than eight in ten adults live beyond sixty-five, and an increasing number are exceeding one hundred years of age. As was stated earlier, there are people alive today who will live to 150 years—and some well beyond that.[40]

Life expectancy is higher in some developed countries.[41] The US is not a leader in life expectancy despite spending more on health care and prevention services than any other country. The developed countries with the longest life expectancy (as of 2015) are:

Country	Life Expectancy	Population in millions
Japan	84.7	126.7M
Italy	82.1	62.0M
Canada	81.8	35.4M
France	81.8	66.8M
Germany	80.5	80.7M

The rate of increase in life expectancy within the United States has been slowing to a point where it is currently stagnant, and some recent trends are indicating that life expectancy in the US is in fact declining. The rate of increase over the past twenty-five years has been at a slower pace than other high-income countries. There are many reasons, but much of this is due to obesity and other destructive habits on health (smoking, drug addiction, deaths from opioid addiction). In a recent analysis of the US population, more than thirteen million people are considered obese. This means that they present a pending major pressure on the national health care system. Further, the lack of access to universal health care services leads Americans to often not treat illnesses until they are chronic. This impacts longevity and the cost of and access to health care.

---

[40] "The First Person to Live to 150 Has Already Been Born—Revisited!" *Forbes*, February 3, 2013.

[41] "Living Longer," paper published by the National Institute on Aging, Bethesda, MD, November 2011.

What Causes Aging?

Each year, we are learning more about what causes aging and what techniques or interventions could extend life. Promising research is being done at Stanford University[42] and Johns Hopkins School of Medicine.[43] They are exploring ways to lengthen telomeres, enzymes that are the timekeepers of cells. When cells divide, telomeres signal the end of the copying process. They are the final segment of the DNA and are at the end of the chromosomes. Shortened telomeres are correlated with many age-related diseases, including heart disease, Alzheimer's, stroke, diabetes, and lung disease. This research may also unlock the reasons why some cells divide indefinitely, creating the condition we call cancer. Researchers are also finding that exercise and other healthy behaviors increase the length of telomeres, and these in turn help telomeres grow.[44]

At the Harvard Stem Cell Institute, scientists have found that there are certain proteins that appear in abundance in younger mice but not in older mice.[45] They are studying whether longer-living humans have more of these proteins than individuals who show age at an earlier time. Researchers at the Glenn Center for Biology of Aging at the University of Michigan[46] and the University of Texas at San Antonio Health Science Center[47] are working on a protein compound called rapamycin. They have found that mice are living 20 percent longer when they take this compound. It seems to slow the aging process. This gene is found in both humans and mice, and it acts to control how cells take in and use energy. It turns out that when these genes turn on cells to consume, the

---

[42]   "Telomere extensions turn back the clock on aging," published by Stanford Medicine News Center, January 22, 2015.

[43]   "Beyond Telomerase," John Hopkins Medicine Publications, November 12, 2015.

[44]   Corey, David, "Telomeres and Telomerase: From Discovery to Clinical Trials," *Chemical Biology*, December 24, 2009.

[45]   Rubin, Lee, PhD and Amy Wagers, PhD, "Functioning of aged brains and muscles in mice made younger," Harvard Stem Cell Institute, May 4, 2014.

[46]   ww.med.umich.edu/geriatrics/research/glenn.

[47]   www.utsystem.edu/institutions/university-texas-health-science-center-san-antonio.

cells age more quickly. They are exploring ways to turn off or moderate this gene that would, as their research is trying to determine, slow the aging process of our cells.

The Human Microbiome Project was established by the National Institutes of Health (NIH) in 2008.[48] Their mission is to understand and generate resources to learn about the microbial communities found in the human body. These communities include bacteria, viruses, eukaryotes, and archaea. There are more than ten times the number of bacteria than cells in the human body. Because of their size, they are only about 1–3 percent of our body mass. Many of these microbes are essential to our health and may produce vitamins and other resources our bodies need as well as teach our immune systems how to recognize and deal with dangerous invaders in our bodies. With the advances in DNA sequencing and genome research, we are learning more about body chemistry than ever before.

Studies regarding the mitochondrial network within the cell are opening up new frontiers of research on longevity. In a study published in *Cell Metabolism*, scientists from the Harvard T. H. Chan School of Public Health report that manipulating this network by dietary restrictions (e.g. fasting) or genetic manipulation may increase the cell's ability to process energy and dramatically extend its life span. Scientists have heretofore not understood why fasting made a difference on health. These studies are showing new causal relationships between diet and cell health.[49] Therefore, these studies indicate that we can achieve longer life by adopting certain dietary behaviors, and there are emerging interventions that may enhance our abilities and expand our longevity.

---

[48]   www.hmpdacc.org.

[49]   Heather J. Weir, Pallas Yao, Frank K. Huynh, Caroline C. Escoubas, Renata L. Goncalves, Kristopher Burkewitz, Raymond Laboy, Matthew D. Hirschey, William B. Mair. "Dietary Restriction and AMPK Increase Lifespan via Mitochondrial Network and Peroxisome Remodeling," *Cell Metabolism,* 2017.

Primary Indicators of Your Health

There are several standard indicators that show overall health. These can be increased or decreased by our actions. We'll examine the indicators and then explore the things you can do to improve the indicators of your well-being and for being well.

An often-cited indicator of your health is your blood pressure. This is simple to test and can be an indicator of the strength and endurance of your heart. The most recent guidelines from the American College of Cardiology and the American Heart Association have lowered the standards for blood pressure from 140/90 to 130/80 (the systolic rating versus the diastolic rating).[50] These were updated in 2017. These new standards were written by a panel of twenty-one scientists and health experts who reviewed more than nine hundred published studies on heart health and blood pressure. This redefined what is considered early-stage hypertension with these lower standards and provides a clear marker for assessing the strength of the heart and risk for heart or cardiovascular disease. Blood pressure does tend to increase as we age. The reason is simple. The arteries become stiff, and this makes the heart work harder to push blood through the system. Monitoring one's blood pressure is often a good motivator for taking actions that both strengthen your heart and keep your circulatory system flexible for as long as possible.

In addition to staying within these blood pressure guidelines, your overall weight and how it is distributed contribute to your longevity and quality of life. The body mass index (BMI) is the estimate of the fat in your body based on your height and weight. BMI that is in the normal range is associated with lower rates of illness and death. The healthy range is between 18.5 and 24.9. The BMI is calculated by dividing your weight in pounds by your height in inches squared (squared = your height inches x your height inches), then multiplying this number by

---

[50] 2017 ACC/AHA/AAPA/ABC/ACPM/AGS/APhA/ASH/ASPC/NMA/PCNA Guideline for the Prevention, Detection, Evaluation, and Management of High Blood Pressure in Adults: A Report of the American College of Cardiology/American Heart Association Task Force on Clinical Practice Guidelines. *J Am Coll Cardiol*, 2017.

703. For example, an individual who weighs 180 pounds and is six-foot-tall would have a BMI of 24.4 (180 lbs. divided by 5,184 (72" x 72") then multiplied by 703 = 24.4). If BMI is less than 18.5, the individual is usually considered underweight. If the BMI is between 25.0 and 29.9, the person is considered overweight. If the BMI is 30 or more, the individual is considered obese.

You can also use the formula to calculate your own target weight as well. If you are six feet tall and want a BMI of 22.0 (within the normal range), then your weight should be 162 pounds. (Desired BME: 22 ÷ 703, x 5,184 (height 72" x 72") = 162).

The BMI is only an indicator of health from a weight standpoint. Where the weight is located is also very important. Fat that is generally around the stomach is an indicator of poorer health conditions than weight that is low or high on the body. Subcutaneous fat lies near the surface and is tucked between the abdominal skin and the muscle wall. This is fat that one can easily grab. The second is called visceral fat and lies beneath the muscles and surrounds vital abdominal organs. Measuring your waist is the most reliable way to determine this. The Nurses' Health Study, a major long-term study of health and weight, determined that people who had a waistline that exceeded thirty-five inches for women and forty inches for men had a higher risk of dying from heart disease or cancer or dying prematurely from any cause. This is "far more dangerous than subcutaneous fat because it isn't just a storage depot for calories. It actually produces compounds that contribute to insulin resistance, lipid imbalances (like too much harmful LDL cholesterol and too little helpful HDL cholesterol), and inflammation, all of which fuel heart disease, type 2 diabetes, and certain forms of cancer."[51]

Cholesterol has been known for many years to have an impact on overall health. In recent years, the assumption that high cholesterol will lead to heart disease is being challenged. Some studies have shown that there is little correlation between high cholesterol and heart disease. Actually, the findings are more complicated. Cholesterol is a waxy

---

[51]   "Living Better, Living Longer," Special Report from the Harvard Medical School, Robert Schneiber, MD, Medical Editor, Anne Underwood Executive Editor, Bolvoir Medical Group, Norwalk, CT, 2017.

substance that is either produced by your liver or comes from food you eat that is high in saturated or trans fats (meat, poultry, certain dairy products, etc.). Your body needs a certain amount of cholesterol, and the liver usually produces all that is needed. When too much is either produced or consumed, it forms thick, hard deposits in your arteries, making them less flexible and less able to transport blood through your system. If a clot forms and blocks a narrowed artery, a heart attack or stroke can result. High cholesterol is a controllable risk, and if it is not managed or is combined with other risk factors (smoking, high blood pressure, diabetes), then the risk of a severe health event becomes even greater.

Cholesterol is measured by rating three elements—LDL (low-density lipoprotein or "bad" cholesterol), HDL (high-density lipoprotein or "good" cholesterol), and triglycerides. Triglycerides are a type of fat that is produced by the liver and is stored all over your body as a source of energy. Too many triglycerides may increase your risk of heart disease. LDL are the fats that cling to artery walls, and HDL are the fats that actually clean LDL from the artery walls.

Total cholesterol level that is less than 180–200 milligrams per deciliter (mg/dL) for individuals over twenty-one years old is generally viewed as desirable for healthy adults. A reading that is 200–239 mg/dL is considered borderline high, and above 240 is considered too high. The individual readings of LDL, HDL, and triglycerides are more important than the overall number. LDL should be less than 100 mg/dL. When LDL is 100–129 mg/dL, this is acceptable if the person has no other health or risk issues. A reading of 130–159 mg/dL is borderline high, and 160–189 mg/dL is high. Above 190 mg/dL is considered at risk and very high. For HDL, the higher the number the better. An HDL reading of below 40 mg/dL for men and 50 mg/dL for women is considered a health risk factor. A reading of 41–59 mg/dL is considered borderline risk, and readings of 60 mg/dL and higher are considered healthy. For triglycerides, levels below 150 are considered healthy, above 150 mg/dL are considered borderline, and above 200 mg/dL needs to be treated.[52]

Stress has been shown as a factor that increases aging and disease. Chronic inflammation is being found as a cause for both aging and the

---

[52] "Cholesterol Guidelines and Heart Health, published by Cleveland Clinic, August 17, 2017.

pain associated with getting older. In many cases, inflammation is caused by stress, which is a natural process of the body's reaction to threats. When the mind senses the body is under attack—whether physically or emotionally—the brain sends signals to the adrenal glands to increase the hormones epinephrine and cortisol, which in turn signals the immune system to release cytokines. This prepares the body to fight an injury or wound. This is the stress response of the human body system and is based on our earliest days as humans (and as animals). If there is no battle, wound, or injury, then the body is flooded with inflammation chemicals. This then creates an environment that encourages brain deterioration, cardiovascular disease, cancer, and other age-related diseases. Chronic stress that is caused by emotional issues has been shown to wear away telomeres and consequently create many age-related challenges.

Your mental mind-set or orientation to life is shown to have an increasingly important impact on your overall health. Simply stated, optimism works to keep you healthy. In a major study of 97,253 women over the age of fifty, those who were optimistic and hopeful about life showed significantly lower rates of heart disease, cancer, and mortality than women who viewed life pessimistically.[53] A similar study in 2012 of 197 people who had recently undergone coronary-bypass surgery found that those who were optimistic had significantly lower complications and re-hospitalization rates than the pessimistic group.[54]

What You Can Do to Live Longer and Live Better

As referenced in the preceding sections of this chapter, there is a lot of research and analysis going on to study the aging factors and develop pathways to extend life and the quality of life. If you apply these research findings, there are many clear actions you can take to improve your health and the quality of your life. By quality, I mean the physical and

---

[53]   Bushak, Lecia, "Optimism vs. Pessimism: Which Is Better For Your Health And Longevity?" *Medical Daily*, April 25, 2014.

[54]   Ronaldson, Amy, et.al "Optimism measured pre-operatively is associated with reduced pain intensity and physical symptom reporting after coronary artery bypass graft surgery," *Journal of Psychosomatic Research*, Vol 77, October 2014.

emotional conditions in which you live. By action, I mean things you can do every day, every week, that slow the natural aging process. There are three definitive areas that can impact your capabilities and longevity. Let's examine them and what you can do to improve your health.

You Are What You Eat

Perhaps the best place to start is with what you eat. What and how much people eat does matter. The US Department of Agriculture (USDA) has conducted and sponsored significant research on the ideal calorie intake for an American. They developed guidelines by age and by level of activity (sedentary, moderately active, and active). An excerpt of these guidelines (www.USDA.gov/healthyguidelines) is shown below:

Males				Females			
Age	Sedentary	Moderately Active	Active	Age	Sedentary	Moderately Active	Active
55 - 60	2,000	2,400	2,600	55 - 60	1,600	1,800	2,200
61 - 65	2,000	2,400	2,600	61 - 65	1,600	1,800	2,000
66 - 70	2,000	2,200	2,600	66 - 70	1,600	1,800	2,000
71 - 75	2,000	2,200	2,600	71 - 75	1,600	1,800	2,000
76 and up	2,000	2,200	2,400	76 and up	1,600	1,800	2,000

The number of calories for an adult male at this stage should be between 2,000 and 2,400 per day; for women, it is between 1,600 and 2,000. This four hundred-calorie range is based on the level of activity you are engaged in every day, but these calories need to come from certain sources to be helpful to the body. If you can reduce this amount by 25 percent, you will have a leaner body, which has all sorts of health and personal benefits. The most important elements of this diet are fresh vegetables, fresh fruits, whole grains, and on occasion a glass of wine.

The USDA recommends between five and nine servings of fruits and vegetables daily. A serving size of vegetables is one cup of cooked or raw vegetables or two cups of leafy vegetables you use in a salad. A medium piece of fruit or half a cup of fruit counts as a fruit serving. So, imagine you have a serving of fruit and juice in the morning, a large salad with some additional vegetables for lunch, and two or three servings of vegetables plus some appropriate protein for your evening meal. Instead of a cookie or a bag of chips in the afternoon, have an apple. Getting to five to nine servings of fruits and vegetables is really not that hard if you put some thought into it.

Protein is a building block in the body's chemistry. It helps to support muscles, bones, energy, and your immune system. There is some controversy about how much protein someone should eat at this stage of life. The Center for Disease Control encourages adults to have no more than 10–30 percent of their daily calories from foods containing protein. This is about forty-six grams of protein for women and fifty-six grams of protein for men. People, however, tend to eat more than they need. To calculate the amount of protein that is right for you, you need seven grams of protein for every twenty pounds of your body weight. For example, if you weigh 120 pounds, you need forty-two grams of protein in your daily diet (120 ÷ 20 = 6, 6 x 7 = 42). If you weigh two hundred pounds, you need seventy grams (200 ÷ 20 = 10, 10 x 7 = 70). A three-ounce piece of meat has approximately twenty-one grams of protein; a large egg has about six grams of protein; a three-and-a-half-ounce fish fillet has about twenty-two grams of protein; one cup of yogurt has eight to twelve grams of protein. Six ounces of tuna or roasted chicken, a cup of rice, a cup of yogurt, and a serving of broccoli together is more than sixty ounces of protein. Hence, in most meals, you can easily obtain the necessary protein. Unfortunately, meals that are heavy in meats are also heavy in fats. Protein-enriched plants such as beans, nuts, or whole grains will give you sufficient protein without the undesired fats. Try to avoid smoked, cured, or processed meats such as bacon or sausage as much as possible.[55]

The American Heart Association recommends using no more than one teaspoon of salt a day. Salt is usually heavily used in processed meats, foods, and meals. You can reduce your use of salt by preparing your own meals and using herbs and spices.[56] One needs to be cautious that when they dine out, many restaurants make heavy use of salt

---

[55] "Living Better, Living Longer," 2017.

[56] "Living Better, Living Longer," Special Report from the Harvard Medical School, Robert Schneiber, MD, Medical Editor, Anne Underwood Executive Editor, Bolvoir Medical Group, Norwalk, CT, 2017.

because it adds to the flavor of the food. They are less concerned with your health than they are about your sense of pleasure from the meal.

Sugar is a major factor that creates health risks. A person can handle a normal amount of sugar as part of the metabolic homeostasis. This is about 10% of one's total calorie intake during the day. For a person eating 2,000 calories, this would equal about 50 grams of sugar per day from all sources – natural and added. You should read the labels of foods and you will likely be very surprised about the amount of sugar you are putting into your body system.

For a calculation of the amount of calories, vitamins, and minerals you need, go to the US Department of Agriculture, and use their interactive calculator: www.nal.usda.gov/fnic/interactiveDRI. There are phone apps that can help you measure, track, and monitor your calorie intake. It is beyond the scope of this book to review them, but I suggest doing some research and finding a program that works for you.

A study published in 2015 of 450,000 European adults found that those whose diet was 70 percent based on plants—fruits, vegetables, nuts, whole grains, and beans—had a 20 percent lower risk of dying from cardiovascular disease that those with a more standard diet. In a 2014 study by the Harvard-affiliated Brigham and Women's Hospital, researchers analyzed data from 4,676 healthy women as part of the Nurses' Health Study and found that those who had a greater adherence to the Mediterranean diet were associated with longer cell telomeres. "Women who followed this diet were biologically younger than those who hadn't."[57]

In a 2009 study of 7,447 people who were at high risk of heart disease, researchers found that individuals who followed the Mediterranean diet had a 30 percent lower incidence of heart attack or stroke than others who follow normal diets after about five years. This was published in the *New England Journal of Medicine* in 2013.[58] Further, the Mayo Clinic

---

[57] "Study Links Mediterranean diet to Longevity in Women," Harvard Women's Health Watch, January 2015.

[58] "Primary Prevention of Cardiovascular Disease with a Mediterranean Diet," *New England Journal of Medicine*, April 4, 2013, Vol. 368, No. 14.

has conducted and published research on this diet plan and shows how it has significant health benefits.[59]

As discussed above, the Mediterranean diet[60] has been shown to have very favorable impact on your health and well-being. The following shows the key elements of a healthy and enjoyable diet:

- Eat an average of five to nine servings of fruits and vegetables per day (an average of two per meal plus a healthy fruit snack).
- Eat whole grain bread and use olive oil instead of butter or margarine; eat whole grain cereals or pasta.
- Have a handful of tree-sourced nuts (such as six to eight almonds, cashews, pistachios, or walnuts) per day (avoid candied, honey-roasted, or salted nuts).
- Enjoy fatty fish (such as mackerel, trout, herring, albacore tuna, or salmon) at least twice per week.
- Enjoy a moderate use of wine, red is preferred, one or two glasses per meal.
- Limit dairy products to 1 percent or fat-free milk, cheese, and ice cream (or try coconut, almond or cashew-based milk) or use an alternative coconut and/or almond milk.
- Substitute monounsaturated fats such as canola oil or olive oil in place of animal fats.
- Substitute herbs and spices in place of salt.
- Minimize sugar intakes, especially from processed or prepared foods and snacks.
- Avoid diet drinks, there is some research showing a link between these sodas and cardiovascular issues – heart attack, stroke, obesity, Type 2 diabetes.[61]
- Limit red meat to less than two or three times per month (keep it lean and avoid sausage, bacon, and other high-fat meats).

---

[59] "Mediterranean Diet: A Heart-Healthy Eating Plan," by the Mayo Clinic Staff, May 2016.

[60] www.mediterraneandiet.com.

[61] Calderone, Julia, "The Mounting Evidence Against Diet Sodas," *Consumer Reports*, May 24, 2017

In addition, a research project often called the "Blue Zones" examined the lifestyles of people in communities where many lived well beyond one hundred years.[62] Dan Buettner led a research team that studied communities throughout the world and found five communities where individuals had the longest life spans. Then, they conducted research on their eating habits, level of exercise and activity, family and community relationships, and other lifestyle issues to determine why they live as long as they do. The five locations are:

- Barbagia region of Sardinia in Italy
- Okinawa in Japan
- Loma Linda in California
- Nicoya Peninsula in Costa Rica
- Ikaria in Greece

The Blue Zone research findings reinforces much of what has been learned about a healthy lifestyle.[63] One of the lessons learned is that individuals who live long and enjoyable lives stop eating when they are no longer hungry as opposed to those who eat until they felt full or the large plate is clean. They suggest stopping eating when they are 80 percent full (not 100 percent). The American tradition is to eat large portions, clear the plate, and eat until you feel full. It takes time for your stomach to signal the brain that it is full. Hence, people often over eat if they wait until they feel full.

The researchers also found that the utensils, plates, bowls, and glasses used by the centenarians were much smaller than those used in the average American household. Consequently, the portions were smaller. This meant that individuals had the satisfaction of finishing a nice meal, with a clean plate, but the plates were often 20–30 percent smaller than those in the US, and this resulted in people in these Blue Zones just eating less. Consequently, they consumed fewer calories and had leaner, healthier bodies.

In some of the more advanced societies, researchers found that individuals in the Blue Zone weighed themselves every day. This meant that people understood where they were from a weight perspective, and

---

[62]   Buettner, Dan, "The Blue Zones: 9 Lessons for Living Longer," *National Geographic*, Washington, DC, 2008.

[63]   www.Bluezone.com

by doing this every day, they made small adjustments when they saw their weight was getting out of line with their desires. And by doing this daily, much of the emotional impact of seeing one's weight was diminished; it was just a daily routine that often guided their eating habits for the day. This is a small but very interesting and easy idea to manage one's weight.

When you eat matters as well. Most of your calories should be consumed before 2:00 p.m. (14:00 hours). Any carbohydrates eaten early in the day are used as fuel for your activities for the next three to four hours after the meal. If they are not used, this material is stored in fat cells. Consequently, it is recommended that your calorie intake achieve a balance of 25 percent at breakfast, 50 percent at lunch, and 25 percent at dinner.[64] Alternatively, the value of intermittent fasting is becoming better known. This process encourages you to eat within an eight-hour time period, and then let your body rest, refresh during the other sixteen hours (when it is not digesting food). This implies you would eat your meals between 8:00 AM (8:00 hours) and 3:00 PM (15:00 hours) or between 12:00 AM (12:00 hours) and 8:00 PM (18:00 hours). It is very important not to eat past 9:00 p.m. (2100 hours) because the food has limited value to your body. It may bring pleasure to your mind but be cautious about what you eat when you don't need the food. So, this means that midnight snacks should be avoided unless you are over ninety, in which case, it doesn't matter—you've lived this long and deserve it, unless your goal is to live to 150.

There are many food sensitivities that have serious impacts on your body. There are individuals who are lactose intolerant and cannot digest milk-based (from cows) products. Children and some adults are seriously sensitive to peanuts and other legumes, which can result in death. Many adults cannot eat shellfish, and some cannot eat any fish without a serious digestive reaction. Finally, there are many children and adults with celiac disease who must pursue a gluten-free diet. While gluten sensitivity is difficult to diagnose, it is believed that between 0.6 percent (6 in every 1,000 people) and 6 percent (6 in every 100 people—this would be twenty million people in the US) have gluten sensitivity. Celiac disease is a genetic autoimmune disorder resulting in serious damage to one's small intestines and other digestive conditions. This sometimes occurs

---

[64]   Freuman, T.D., "What You Eat Matters. Does When You Eat Matter Too?" *US News*, Jan. 20, 2015.

when eating foods with gluten, a protein found in wheat, barley, rye, and other grains. The reasons why this occurs is not clear, and there is much research being conducted in diagnosing and seeking cures. When someone with celiac disease eats such proteins, the body overreacts, and this damages the villi, fingerlike parts of the small intestines that absorb foods needed for your nourishment. The results can be the inability to absorb nutrients, vomiting, abdominal pain, diarrhea, gas, constipation, bone loss, and many other related symptoms. The symptoms for celiac disease are not always noticeable. People with celiac also often have deficiencies in iron, Vitamin B12, Folate and Vitamin D. If this is your condition, have yourself tested for celiac disease.

Since food is a fundamental requirement for living, we often are what we eat. Care must be taken to find the right balance between food that is pleasurable and food that is necessary to sustain and help our bodies function properly. If you have any of the allergies mentioned above, then it is important to find a diet and preparation style that fits well with your lifestyle. There are those who eat to live, and others who live to eat. Which one are you?

Don't Just Sit There, Do Something

The documentation and understanding of the impact of exercise on health is very clear and very compelling. Physical fitness appears to slow normal age-related shrinkage of the brain. Exercise appears to strengthen the hippocampus, a brain structure important for memory. It also encourages the development of new blood vessels in the brain and the delivery of oxygen and vital nutrients. There is also evidence that exercise causes the formation of new connections between brain cells and increases the level of neurotrophins that nourish brain cells and help protect them from the damage of stroke and other injuries.

According to a 2017 study, after a six-month aerobic exercise program with people in their sixties and seventies, they improved their cardiovascular fitness and performance on a range of cognitive tasks. "People who increased their physical activity after midlife had an 81 percent lower risk of developing dementia than those who stayed sedentary, and the impact of exercise was greatest in those who were overweight or obese."[65] The process is called *neurogenesis*. People who begin an exercise program in their sixties can reduce the risk of dementia by more than 50 percent.[66] This is shown on the following chart:

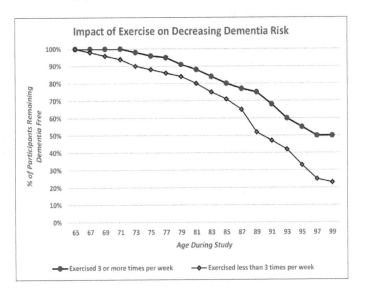

Diet and exercise are interdependent in how they impact your health. There is fascinating research showing that sugars and carbohydrates are more harmful to you than fats. High blood sugar levels appear to do more damage to the cells throughout the body, which is why diabetes is such a horrific disease. The stomach and small intestines break down all foods into digestible particles. When you eat foods high in sugars, starches, or carbohydrates, they are absorbed into the blood, and this elevates your blood sugar. The pancreas responds by releasing insulin, which in turn moves blood glucose into cells of non-exercising muscles and fat cells where it is either used for energy or stored as fat. Exercising will move the blood sugar into the muscles without insulin needed to moderate the rise. Without exercise, insulin is elevated, and fat cells increase. When exercising, you decrease the carbohydrates stored in your muscles (glycogen), and this provides energy needed for the muscle cells. Without a balance between your exercise and your intake of carbohydrates and other calories, you will

---

[65] "Living Better, Living Longer," 2017.

[66] Harety, Barbara Bradley, *Life Reimagined: The Science, Art and Opportunity of Midlife*, Riverhead Books, 2017.

both store the food in fat cells and gain or retain weight.[67] This is why your weight is simply a product of demand versus supply, input versus output, and eating versus exercise.

The challenge is getting into the habit of daily exercising and finding joy and pleasure though these activities. Ideally you would get yourself in to a daily exercise habit, much like you do when you brush your teeth or take a shower or bath. If you work at doing this every day, then when you miss one or two days a week because of other activities or priorities, you still would have exercised at least five times that week.

A useful framework is to organize these activities into three categories. Each of these is intended to develop certain elements of one's physical being; the benefits that are generated for you emotionally and mentally are extra bonuses.

1) Cardiovascular Exercise

This exercise is intended to get your heart rate at a level that strengthens the heart muscle, expands lung capacity, and burns the food supplies that you have taken in. This is moderate exercise for twenty or thirty minutes. Moderate is when you're really working, huffing and puffing, sweating, and able to talk only in short sentences. Vigorous exercise includes some of the same work as moderate, but you can't talk much because you are concentrating more on your exercising than conversation.[68] The goal is to increase your heart rate to be in a zone that is compatible with your age.

According to the Mayo Clinic guidelines,[69] the desired range from minimum to maximum level of heart rate are:

Age	Minimum	Target	Maximum Beats per Minute
55—59	83	140	165
60—64	80	136	160

---

[67] Jakubowicz, D., Barenea M., Wainstein, J., Foy, O., "High caloric intake at breakfast vs. dinner differentially influences weight loss of overweight and obese women." *Obesity Journal*, Dec. 21, 2013 (12), 2504–12.

[68] "Living Better, Living Longer," 2017.

[69] Mayo Clinic website: www.mayoclinic.org.

| 65—69 | 78 | 132 | 155 |
| 70+ | 75 | 128 | 150 |

One should monitor the heart rate periodically during the exercise period and seek to increase the heart rate over time—but do not to exceed the maximum. To determine your heart rate, simply place two fingers from one hand on the underside of your wrist, between the bone and the tendon on the thumb side. When you feel your pulse, count how many beats there are over fifteen seconds. Then, multiply this number by four, and you will have the heart rate. Obviously, these ranges are based on normal body conditioning; very active athletes may have the capacity to achieve higher rates than shown. The goal is to sustain the heart rate in the range appropriate to your age and condition for a twenty to thirty-minute period, and to do this on a daily basis (try for seven days, and you'll likely do five days per week, which is ideal). The good news is that this doesn't need to be done all at one sitting; three ten-minute workout sessions during the day can have the same physical benefit as one thirty-minute workout.[70]

An excellent way to strengthen the heart muscle is with interval training.[71] This is when you work very hard for thirty to sixty seconds, significantly stressing the heart for this period to drive up the heart rate, and then return to standard range for a while during the exercise period. Research has shown that exercises that incorporate interval training provide substantially better health outcomes than maintaining a standard heart rate over the same time period. Interval training is also highly recommended as part of your aerobic exercise program. This is increasing the intensity of your workout for short bursts of time. For example, if you are using a stationary bike or treadmill, after about eight minutes at your normal speed, kick up the intensity so you are going as fast as you can for thirty to sixty seconds, and then return to your normal speed. After another eight minutes, do this again. In a study conducted in 2017, interval training was discovered to boost the activity of mitochondria in muscle cells, which contributed greatly to gaining

---

[70]   "Living Better, Living Longer, 2017.
[71]   "Interval Training for a Stronger Heart" published by Harvard Health Publishing, Harvard Medical School, August 2015.

desired muscle mass. It worked better in older adults than younger adults.[72] However, like all exercise programs, you should consult a professional trainer or physician for a program that is best suited to your particular situation, condition, and goals.

2) Strengthening Exercise

These are exercises that strengthen your muscles in all areas of your body. As we age, our muscles tend to become thinner and weaker. Your goal is to create strong muscle mass within your body. This can be accomplished by doing rigorous muscle-building sessions two to three per week (at least every other day). It is important to include exercises in these muscle groups: legs, hips, back, chest, abdomen, arms, and shoulders. The exercise period should last at least twenty minutes. This includes lifting weights and doing exercises that put pressure on specific muscle groups. The key is to strengthen your core muscles, including the abdominal, back, and pelvic muscle groups. Exercises that strengthen your arms and legs provide a full workout to tone the body and enhance your strength and appearance. Some of these strengthening exercises are achieved by doing yoga or working with weights at a gym or in your home. This process will help you preserve and strengthen your muscle mass at any age—and also give you a better appearance.

3) Balance and Stretching

These exercises create greater flexibility and reduce the chances of injury during other exercises. Doing light stretching for five or ten minutes before aerobic exercises warms the muscles and prepares the body for a more effective workout. It is most important to do these exercises during and at the end of a workout involving aerobic and strengthening exercises to fully stretch and cool down the muscles. This will often reduce soreness and injury. Improving your balance can be as easy as standing on one foot for at least twenty-five seconds and perhaps doing this when your eyes are closed. If one does yoga, Pilates, or Tai

---

[72]   "Living Better, Living Longer," 2017

Chi, then balance and strengthening exercises are incorporated into the exercise routine. This process should not be uncomfortable or painful, and it should deepen your breathing, focus, balance, and concentration. This will make your muscles more flexible, responsive, and diminish pain and injury.[73]

Just Help Yourself

Each person is different, and your plan to remain healthy should reflect what you like doing and what is good for you. In addition to the right balance of diet and exercise, you should identify a few things that work for you to keep healthy. Some of these are listed below.

1) Meditation and Mindfulness

One of the best ways to reduce stress is through meditation and mindfulness exercises. Studies at the Center for Investigating Healthy Minds at the University of Wisconsin at Madison have shown that regular practice of contemplative methods of being reduces cytokines and other inflammation factors and the decline in brain functions.[74] This is the process of closing your eyes, focusing on your breath, and being still. Your mind may wander, and your task is to let it go and just keep returning to your breath.

With special training and practice, this daily ritual of approximately twenty minutes will have enormous benefits to your health and well-being. Meditation reduces stress, which has multiple benefits (reduced inflammation, increased mental alertness and acuity, etc.). This is something that you can do on your own, but it is often best to be trained by a professional. There are also many apps for your smartphone that can be downloaded and used to support your meditation program.

---

[73] An excellent resource is published by the Harvard University Medical School, entitled "Starting to Exercise" (Howard Hartley and I-Min Lee, 2015).

[74] Rosenbranz, Melissa, PhD, "A comparison of mindfulness-based stress reduction and an active control in modulation of neurogenic inflammation," *Brain, Behavior and Immunity*, Vol, 27, January 2013.

Make this an important part of your daily routine. Managing your stress is perhaps one of the most important things you can do to remain healthy. Being self-compassionate, appreciative, and positive are critical attributes of a healthy person.[75]

2) Supplemental Vitamins

While most of your nutrition should come from the foods you eat, it is often helpful to take additional vitamins. Be careful and consult a nutritionist, dietician, or holistic health professional about what types and amounts you should take. There are a lot of scams when it comes to dietary supplements. There are new organizations providing recommendations for vitamins that are designed specifically for your current health conditions and DNA. Those that are based on real science and analysis can help you take the right type and amounts of vitamins to strengthen your health system. Research them carefully since they may offer some important guidance on what will be best for you. This is part of a major medical trend to personalize treatments rather than just taking standard, universally applied treatments. These are customized to your unique body chemistry and needs. Two outstanding sources are Rootine Vitamins (www.rootinevitamins.com) and Weil Vitamin Advisor (www. Weilvitaminadvisor.com). Both organizations conduct an analysis of your body characteristics and practices to develop personalized servings that fits what you need. Rootine Vitamins uses an analysis of your DNA and blood tests to develop its vitamin protocol. Weil uses questions and your descriptions of your activities. Both will provide the vitamin mix you need, which is how they make their income.

There are disagreements in medical sciences about which and how many vitamins you need, but here are a few suggested vitamins that may help for specific needs:

---

[75]   "Living Better, Living Longer," 2017.

- **Omega-3**

This vitamin assists in reducing inflammation and adds oils needed to improve your body's functions in many areas. This vitamin oil reduces plaque buildup in the arteries, keeps blood sugar levels in check, and improves brain functioning. The recommended dose is 1,000 mg per day.[76]

- **Vitamin D**

This helps supplement what you get from the sun. Some scientists believe vitamin D helps reduce the risks of cancer and osteoporosis. There is some controversy regarding whether this vitamin will strengthen your immune system, so depending on your situation, this is worth some additional research on your part. The recommended dose is six hundred international units per day.[77]

- **Vitamin B12**

This helps prevent dementia and supports your digestive system in processing foods and maximizing the values of the foods you eat. The recommended dose is 2.4 micrograms per day.[78]

- **Vitamin C**

This is another common and often very helpful supplement if needed. It supports the body's growth, development, and repair of all body tissues. It supports many functions, including collagen, wound healing, absorption of iron, and helps build strong teeth, bones, and cartilage. The recommended dose is 90 mg for men and 75 mg for women.

---

[76] Paturel, Amy, "Supplements to Take in Your 50s, 60s, and 70s," *AARP Magazine*, December 2014.

[77] Nutrition Source: Vitamin D and Health, Harvard School of Public Health.

[78] Paturel, Amy, op. cit.

• Probiotics

The body's digestive system needs bacteria to function effectively. Without healthy gut bacteria, the body cannot break down foods, absorb nutrients, and support growth. Since each body system is somewhat different, it is unclear which probiotics are best suited to your unique conditions. The recommended dose is 1–10 billion CFUs a few days per week. These are particularly important after you have been on a regimen of antibiotics for an illness because your gut bacteria need to be restored to perform their healthy functions.[79]

• Flaxseeds

When taken as supplements with food (as ground seeds, not oil), flaxseeds have been shown to have a very positive impact on strengthening the immune system, reducing cancer, and improving heart functions. Too much flaxseed can cause digestive problems, so the amount should be determined with your physician or health advisor.[80]

• Calcium

Women in particular often need supplements of calcium to prevent bone loss. This may be helpful for men if bone health is a problem. The recommended dose is 1,000 mg for men and 1,200 mg for women, split into two daily doses.[81]

Before you add supplements to your diet, be sure to check out some of the latest research on alternative medicines. A good source is the National Center for Complementary and Integrative Health (www.

---

[79]   Paturel, Amy, op. cit.

[80]   Nordqvist, Joseph, "Flaxseed: How Healthful Is It?" *Medical News Today*, March 2017.

[81]   "Calcium and calcium supplements: Achieving the right balance" published by the Mayo Clinic, *Nutrition and Healthy Eating*.

nccih.nih.gov/health). Also check out *Consumer Reports* for some of their latest research and product assessments.[82]

3) Adapt to changes in your sexual drive and abilities.

Both men and women go through significant changes in sexual drive (libido) and capabilities as they age. Men are likely to face erectile dysfunction, times when they are not able to get or maintain an erection, or having trouble reaching an orgasm. Their testosterone levels decline, and cardiovascular problems (including vascular leakage) may increase as they age. Taking testosterone supplements may help, but they also may increase the risk of prostate cancer. Check with your physician and monitor your PSA (the test for prostate cancer) before you use supplements. Women often find that the vagina becomes drier, have thinning of tissue (vaginal atrophy), or experience real pain when having intercourse.

Men and women lose sensitivity, which appears to accelerate between the ages of sixty-five and seventy-five. This can result in difficulties in reaching orgasm even though the mind and emotional conditions are ready. All this results in less frequent sex and may create worry by one or both parties that something is wrong in their relationship. Many of these changes are the product of our aging bodies and not because of a decline in affection or attraction to the other partner.

It is often important for each person to see a physician to diagnose and discuss the situation and potential solutions. If this is an issue in your relationship, talk about it and bring your questions to a therapist or physician who may provide helpful information and insights that reduce your concerns and worries. There are many options available now, and a physician or a therapist can often assist in providing good solutions. Sharing your experiences and concerns with each other is also very important for sustaining the relationship. This can help recalibrate expectations and reinforce the intimacy needed in every relationship.

---

[82] "Natural Cures: Your A–Z Guide," *Consumer Reports*, November 2018.

4) Look for ways to boost your immune system.

Much of the research shows the importance of a strong immune system. What is clear is that exercise does a great deal to make you stronger—not just with your muscles but with your immune system. Certain vitamins and minerals noted above will also improve your internal strength. Building a strong immune system should be a top priority as you age.

5) Strengthen your brain.

While there are many purported medicines and exercises that will strengthen the memory and brain, be sure to check the validity of the research before purchasing these products. Intellectual and learning stimulations help create more brain connections and increase the density of synapse (the connections between the brain cells). Remember that exercises may have the greatest impact on your brain's health. Some of the activities[83] that have been shown as effective are:

- **Learn a language.**

In a 2016 study, people (average age fifty) who took an intensive one-week language course improved their ability to sustain, focus, and shift their attention, and the benefits were still apparent nine months later in all of those who kept practicing at least five hours a week. Those who took other types of courses didn't show the same improvement. Many individuals are traveling to other countries to immerse themselves in a new language, and when they get home, they take classes or work with a tutor to sustain and deepen their skills.

- **Play music.**

Musicians appear to have stronger brain capacity for making quick decisions and other executive functions of the brain. Playing an

---

[83]   "Living Better, Living Longer," 2017.

instrument and singing have several positive stimulating effects on the brain and its functions.

- **Stay socially active.**

Research is also showing that people who are socially engaged have better memories and other cognitive abilities than those who are more reclusive. Playing games like bridge and other mentally challenging games combine socializing with friends and a strong cognitive workout.

6) See a chiropractor and/or an acupuncturist.

Chiropractic medicine began in the late nineteenth century. For years, it was considered an approach to natural healing. Over the past several decades, chiropractors have focused on spinal alignment and have recently returned to some of its roots in natural healing and more holistic health.

Acupuncturists, like chiropractors, do not have their roots in Western medicine. Acupuncture has been around for centuries and has proven to have great benefits to some diseases and promotes good health. My intent here is to neither promote nor discourage these disciplines. You should explore and decide for yourself with proper advice and counsel. For one, I have received great benefits from both.

7) Minimize sugar in your diet – both processed and natural

Sugar is found in many processed foods and beverages. Dietary Guidelines indicate that we should consume no more than 10% of our daily calories from sugar. One 16 oz. can of soda, for example, contains 52 grams of sugar which is more than recommended for the average person for the entire day. Consuming fructose, which is the main source of sugar, increases your hunger for more foods and leads to obesity and visceral fat accumulation. This results in higher risks of heart disease, inflammation, triglycerides and blood pressure. Studies have shown that sugar also increases the risks of cancer, depression, cognition decline as well as accelerates aging of the skin and general cells.[84] Artificial sweeteners, while cutting down on calories, impacts the good gut bacteria causing people to eat more not less. While sweets are often good and satisfying, getting your sweets from fruits is better than from candy. Unfortunately, we often associated sweets with rewards. Being thoughtful about how and how much you eat is important to your health. And like many of our food guidelines, all things should be in moderation.

8) Consider doing a cleanse diet.

When working with a natural health professional, you may participate in a cleanse diet and restrict certain foods (meats, dairy, or grains) for thirty days or longer. *The Whole 30 Diet* walks you through a diet regime over a thirty-day period of time, and you eliminate sugars, dairy, and grains from your diet for only thirty days. There are many physical and mental changes that occur during this time period and doing these changes for this time period may change the way you eat certain things for the rest of your life. The key benefit of these programs is how they reduce much of the toxins that build up over time and help the body restart important healthy functions. Research this carefully before you participate in one of these programs, but they can have significant benefits.[85] [86]

9) Try intermittent fasting.

Fasting has been very popular for centuries. The theory (and there is increasing science to support this) is that fasting places stress on the body system that will cause it to kick into rapid production of new cells. It enables the body to use the stored energy and repair itself during times

---

[84]   Shan Luo, J. Monterosso, K. Sarpelleh, K. Page, "Differential effects of fructose versus glucose on brain and appetitive responses to food cues and decisions for food rewards" *Proc Natl Acad Sci U S A*, 2015 May 19; 112(20)

[85]   Glass, Jonathan, *Total Life Cleanse*, Healing Arts Press, 2018.

[86]   Hartwig, Melissa, *The Whole 30*, Houghton Mifflin Harcourt, 2015.

when it is not processing your food intake. The newer cells are thought of as healthier, stronger, and more able to improve life. Intermittent fasting is very popular and simple. Essentially, you follow a schedule where you only eat during eight hours of the day (say from noon till 8:00 p.m. or 12:00 and 20:00 hours) and refrain from eating anything during the other times. You may have other long periods during the day when you do not eat or snack. The enables the body's systems to focus on certain things during these cycles—like digesting food during your eating time and repairing and building cells when you are not eating. It is important to consult a professional before you begin such a regime and use creative ways to eat better foods during your eating periods. Your body will appreciate this care you are taking.

10) It is time to stop addictive behaviors.

As hard as these are to stop, there are many people who are addicted to smoking, alcohol, drugs, and medicines, putting themselves into programs that lead them away from these destructive behaviors. If this is you, these actions will give you your life back. There is evidence that after just one year of not smoking, your risk of a heart attack decreases by 50 percent. So, the damage can likely be reversed. Find and use the help you need and be good to yourself. You deserve this. There are many tools and aids available to reduce dependency on nicotine, drugs, and alcohol and put them into your past. You are not alone. Every day that you continue with addictive behaviors takes time off your life and lessens your ability to be there with and for others. You don't need to feel judged; you already know these facts. Consult your physician or talk to your friends or children if you need reasons to stop. There are many ready to help. Your life may simply depend on this.

11) Increase your consumption of water.

Water is essential for good health because it carries nutrients to your cells, promotes a moist environment for your eyes, ears, nose, and throat, and flushes toxins out of vital organs. The customary recommendation is to drink at least eight eight-ounce glasses of water (or other similar fluids) per day. The actual amount depends on your level of exercise and activity, the environment in which you live (hot zones, high altitudes), and your general health conditions. The body is composed of approximately 60 percent water, and this water leaves your body through evaporation, urination, breath, and perspiration. Consequently, the amount should be adjusted based on your use of water. Health professionals recommend that you have a glass of water with each meal, drink before, during, and after you exercise, and then a few other times during the day. Keep a bottle of water with you during they day. You'll be hydrated and this will keep you away from sugar enriched drinks.

Water is inexpensive and refreshing, and it should become your beverage of choice. Most people do not drink enough water. There are few foods that provide as valuable a service to your body as simple water.[87]

12) Get a good night's sleep.

Over the past several years, much research has been done about sleep habits and the value of sleep to a person's health. The National Sleep Foundation has found that getting less than six hours of sleep per night doubles the risk of a heart attack or stroke. This research recommends that individuals shut off electronics at least an hour before bedtime because the light interferes with resting your brain. The desired range of sleep is between seven and eight hours per night. One may adjust when you go to bed if waking during the night is a customary problem, so that you receive the desired amount of rest.[88] In addition sleep apnea is a sleep disorder that can have serious heart and health consequences. The symptoms are loud snoring, episodes of breathing cessation during sleep, abrupt awakenings with a dry mouth, sore throat, headache, and excessive daytime sleepiness (hypersomnia). This can result in irritability, attention problems, memory loss, and disturbances to your sleep partner. If you face any of these symptoms, see your doctor and

---

[87]   "Water: How Much Should You Drink Every Day?" published by the Mayo Clinic: Nutrition and Healthy Eating

[88]   To learn more about sleep, go to the Harvard Medical School division on "Sleep Medicine," www.sleep.med.harvard.edu.

take the simple overnight sleep exam. A treatment plan has been shown to be highly effective. A good night's sleep is a wonderful thing.

Visions for the Future

There is an emerging field known as geroscience. This is the study and research of science related to aging. Some of the researchers are studying the habits and bodies of centenarians (those who live past one hundred) and supercentenarians (those who live past 110). One of the goals is to extend the period of time one experiences the Consolidation stage and help people live healthier and independent lives longer—until they reach the Final stage. Unfortunately, most grants for this type of research are based around a particular disease, including cancer, heart disease, diabetes, and Alzheimer's. Of the major national research centers, only the National Institute on Aging[89] is focused on aging, and it is working to take a more holistic view of the causes and cures for age-related diseases.

Some of the new breakthroughs in medical science are being done at the Broad Institute in Cambridge, Massachusetts (www.broadinstitute. org). This is the organization that led the coding and documentation of the human gene and has made this available to researchers throughout the world. This work alone has been revolutionary. A team of scientists lead by Feng Zhang is conducting research on a system call CRISPR (clustered regularly interspaced short palindromic repeats). CRISPR is a bacterial defense system that enables scientists to edit the DNA strand that exists in every cell. There are more than six thousand gene-based diseases, and these diseases are caused by mutations of the sequence of the DNA. With CRISPR, scientists believe they can cut out the impaired portion of the DNA that is causing the health problem and replace it with a healthy sequence. With these systems, scientists can modify the genetic code of the DNA in exact locations in order to treat the disease caused by the genetic sequence. This is increasing the speed with which they can do remarkable research on the disease and health at the molecular level of the cell.

---

[89] www.nia.nih.gov

CRISPRs were first discovered by Francisco Majica, a scientist at the University of Alicante in Spain. In 2007, his theory about using CRISPRs as part of the bacterial immune system was experimentally demonstrated. Feng Zhang at the Broad Institute has been promoting and training researchers all over the world to understand, share their findings, and develop new applications for the CRISPR system. It was also featured on *60 Minutes*[90] and is offering some exciting strategies for the prevention and treatment of genetic-based diseases.

Let us also consider the projections of Dr. Ray Kurzweil.[91] In *The Singularity is Near*, Dr. Kurzweil discusses the evolution of biology and technology from the beginning of time, and he draws forecasts based on ever-increasing technology capabilities. If you consider the process of change since the beginning of life forms, we are facing an exponentially increasing rate of change. There will be a point in time, according to Dr. Kurzweil, where technology will become smarter than humans, and we will physically merge with technology. The point where one cannot differentiate between biological and technological beings is called the "singularity." According to Kurzweil, since technology does not die like biological material, humankind will live forever.

While one may consider this view outrageous, consider that the first artificial heart was successfully implanted by Dr. Robert Jarvick to Barney Clark in 1982. According to the National Centers for Health Statistics, joint replacements (knee and hip) have increased from 138,700 in 2000 to 310,800 in 2010. Further, 80,000 joint replacements were made by individuals over seventy-five. And the hospital stay has reduced from more than five days to four or fewer.[92] Consider all the individuals who have returned from the wars in Iraq and Afghanistan or who have been in horrible accidents and lost limbs. Today, many

---

[90]   https://www.cbsnews.com/news/crispr-the-gene-editing-tool-revolutionizing-biomedical-research

[91]   Kurzweil, Ray, *The Singularity Is Near,* Penguin Books, 2006.

[92]   Mark Pagnano, MD, professor and chairman, department of orthopedic surgery, Mayo Clinic, Rochester, Minn.; Monica Wolford, M.A., statistician, and Anita Bercovitz, MPH, PhD, health scientist, US National Center for Health Statistics, Hyattsville, Md.; Feb. 12, 2015, *Data brief,* National Center for Health Statistics.

of them are walking, running, throwing baseballs, picking up their kids, and enjoying life because of prosthetics and artificial limbs that communicate the sensation of touch and temperature to the brain, like a biological limb.

But for now, you must take care of yourself. There is no magic medicine or technology that can eliminate what ails you or cure your physical problems. You need to take care of yourself because you are the only one who can do it. It is relatively easy to understand what needs to be done. The most challenging part is modifying behaviors and routines to do these things, on a regular basis, on a sustained basis, so they become habits. This chapter has outlined the actions that can save your life and enable you to enjoy your life to the fullest extent possible. Consider these questions:

- What are your reasons for keeping yourself healthy?
- How important are these to you?
- What are you doing to make yourself healthy and keep yourself healthy?
- What are you doing that is harming your health?
- What can you start doing—or doing more of—today to give you the health and the life you want?
- How can you reinforce these new healthy lifestyle practices so they become characteristic of who you are?

Chapter 8

Who Are You Going to Be?

The greatest potential for growth and self-realization exists in the second half of life.
—Carl Jung

O ne of the most challenging aspects of moving into this next stage—Reinventing Adulthood—is how you describe yourself and what you do. This is not just to others—but to yourself. As you approach this time, you may start to worry about who you are during this time. You will no longer be the _____ (Fill in this blank with your occupation). You can no longer think of yourself as something that you once were. This may be difficult for the ego and self-image to let go. If you are no longer an executive, teacher, consultant, sales leader, technician, or software developer, then who are you?

What do you say when someone asks you, "What do you do?" Is this answer easy or difficult? Do you think of yourself as a retired person, a partially retired person or a "pre-retired" person? What if you started to think of yourself as a traveler, learner, artist, sports activist—or whatever expression captures your new life's work? The importance of this title, description, or label cannot be underestimated to describe who you are or will become. This gives you something different to hold on to and establish as your identity, your brand, and this will define how you choose to live.

Given all the information covered in this book, the focus of this chapter will be on helping you figure out how to redefine your identity and create the lifestyle that reflects this. In the next chapter, you will have a series of exercises and worksheets to build your Master Plan for this next stage. But for now, let's look at who you want to become.

Redefining Your Identity

This is the time to reimagine your life into a new way of being. Many people get stuck with this challenge, and others glide right into a new lifestyle. You may feel a little bit of both. If this is easier, view this next stage in terms of mini-stages, like what you want to do for the next one year or three years. Then, as you approach the end of that time period, you can think about the next three or five years. In my experience, it is difficult to answer broad, general questions like "What are you going to do for the rest of your life?" and easier and more practical to ask time-based questions like "What do you want to do before you turn seventy or seventy-five?"

This is a time in life where you can be free of deadlines, to-do lists, decision pressures, and job responsibilities. Although the Longevity Project cited earlier encourages us to be focused on goals and engaged, this is also a time to define your actions on your own terms. It is time to define how you want to be and what you want to do and follow the things that provide you with the greatest sense of meaning, value, and interest. You can live your life with or without goals, measures of progress, and active pressures to achieve something that is important to others—or you can use them to reinforce your journey. Perhaps this is a time to take a different path to fulfill your purpose. This is the time when you must take the initiative and the responsibility.

In our interview, David said, "As I transition to my next stage, I struggle with the question of how to make this time successful, not in how others see me but in how I see myself. At the end of the day, was it a productive day?"

I found that women tend to have less difficulty in the identity transformation. Anne F. did not let her career define her identity. "When I retired, I wasn't that worried about who I was. I just jumped into it. I see my retirement challenge as doing things that I was afraid of doing."

Your financial condition may place limitations on what you can do. You may need to continue to generate income at least for some time period. Understanding your financial conditions and the impact of this reality will influence your ability to live a secure and comfortable life. Ideally, your financial conditions will fall into the background, and you will adjust your lifestyle to living within your means.

In addition to your purpose and financial condition, relationships take on greater importance. As one moves away from working, relationships start moving into the foreground. People tend to focus their time and attention on relationships with their significant others, core family, grandchildren, and critical friends.

Phil B. said that when his children gave him grandchildren, something magical happened. He said it was hard to describe, but he and his wife's lives have changed fundamentally. Time enables you to spend more of your day with them, and this is important because along with a sense of purpose, relationships build a stronger sense of self. How important are these relationships to your identity?

We have also learned the importance of healthy habits. These are things you can (and should) do regarding your diet, exercise, and other ways of taking care of yourself. These activities are critical to your brain and heart functions, lung capacity, cardiovascular system, immune system, and stress or inflammation within your body. The more you can integrate these into your daily lifestyle, the better you will be able to achieve and fulfill the things you want from this life. What could be more important than this? How do you make these actions part of who you are?

So, the important challenge is to integrate these factors—your sense of purpose, financial capabilities, strong relationships, and healthy habits—into how you describe yourself to others and yourself. You might think of this as your elevator pitch. This is a ten- or fifteen-second statement you say to someone when they ask, "So what do you do for a living?" The blending of these activities into your life is the key to a fulfilling life. This will then provide a new definition of who you are, your sense of identity, and who you might want to become in this next stage of life.

Exploring the Possibilities

A useful way to redefine your identity in this next stage of life is to explore alternative scenarios and determine which sound and feel like something you want. Through my research and interviews, I found ten different models or archetypes, and each has a particularly unique focus and value. There are examples of how people are living each type of lifestyle. There may be many more types of people as well as combinations of what is described. The important point here is to identify and explore the ones that are interesting to you and within the parameters defined by your current (or future) conditions. In so doing, you can discover what you want to become.

When you read the descriptions below, you may find a particular model or a combination of them particularly meaningful and exciting to you. Look at them. Reflect on why these are important to you and how you would feel describing them to others. Think about ways you can describe yourself using one model or a combination of these models and what you want to be known for (to yourself and to others). Look for ways to personalize it to the person you are or want to be. While there are elements you want in each, your task is to determine what best describes what you want to do, be known for and how to create this in this next stage of your life.

1) Working Professional

This person wants to continue working in her or his current role, company, profession, or at something different. You may leave your current employer and join another organization that is more suited to your needs and desired flexibility. You may stay with your current employer but change your role or job. You will continue to earn income; this is not working as a volunteer (this is another lifestyle). There is important research on how individuals want to transition out of their employers. A significant majority of individuals want an "off-ramp" when they leave their organization as opposed to a "cliff drop" into retirement.[93]

If possible, individuals at this life stage could work in their chosen profession for a few hours per day, for three to eight days per month, or perhaps fulltime for a few months during the year. Then, they can pursue other interests or activities and prepare what is needed to leave the employment life. Organizations that value the wisdom and talents of these individuals are adapting work schedules to meet the availability and income needs of these individuals. These organizations view succession as not just who will replace the individual but how both the organization and individual will move through a transition so they both are strengthened.

Larry and Maryanne have had a very successful consulting practice for many years. Though they are both in their seventies, they continue to work and enjoy working with clients and being engaged in assisting the companies they serve. They appreciate the sustained income as well. However, they are starting to scale back from time to time, and they find they are taking more extended vacations associated with attending business meetings and conferences. It is a way to sustain the business, remain engaged, and create opportunities that enrich their lives. They create business opportunities that take them to visit their new grandson.

When Richard left his profession as a scientist, he took a position as an adjunct professor at a local university. He learned how to develop and teach through online courses, and he developed a special curriculum for the university. He enjoyed working with the students and helping them develop their research skills and insights. Many colleges and universities are utilizing highly skilled researchers, executives, and professionals to create classroom experiences and share knowledge and stories with students who are eager to learn from someone who has been there. The compensation of an adjunct professor may not be adequate or reflect the value of one's experience, but these individuals do it anyway. The experience and engagement provide a great deal of the rewards.

---

[93]   Casey, Tom and Karen Warlin, *Executive Transitions: A Guide for Transitioning Executives and Companies That Employ Them*, Telemachus Press, LLC, www.discussionpartners.com, 2013.

Betsy initially got involved doing development and fund-raising for a private school on a volunteer basis. She found she loved the work, and it grew to a paying job and her passion. While she is well past the normal time of retirement, she loves the interaction with the school's administrators, teachers, and supporters. It does not feel like a job, and her experience and energy continue to make a major contribution to the school and help sustain its future.

Eric continues to work as a mediation attorney because he loves it. Several years ago, he and his wife reviewed their financial conditions and discovered that they could afford to retire. However, he loves his work, gets immense satisfaction from the resolution of major issues, and wants to continue working on his terms. He realized that his time was more valuable than money. He also recently became a grandfather, and he said it changed everything. His son recently asked him whether he was doing what he really wanted to be doing. This was an important question that Eric is exploring.

Do you want to pursue the same basic form of work you performed during your working career, do something similar, or do something totally different? A core theme for many is using this time to continue adding value to society and engaging in activities that they dreamed about during an earlier stage. How do you do this and not be exploited by an organization that seeks the depth of experience without paying fairly for the value provided? Again, the important objective of this activity is to keep yourself challenged and your mind sharp, contribute, and if you make some money, all the better. Fairness in pay and work commitments are being redefined and negotiated. We are emerging with a gig economy where talent is employed in many dynamic ways.

2) Advisor/Mentor/Guide/Coach

This is a person who has become an advisor or a guide to others. The primary activities here are similar to a consultant or teacher where you help the other person learn and become more effective or efficient. You do not do their work for them. You may be paid for this role or do this as a volunteer. You may sell or give your time as an advisor or serve on the board of directors for a newly emerging company or a well-established company. You may have authority and fiduciary responsibility or be independent of the organization. You bring your experience and wisdom to the discussions. You bring your caring about the organization and people you serve. You may bring your passion for a sport if you are a coach or personal trainer to a team of kids or adults. The key challenge is to shift your mind-set from doing it (you may think that you could do this much faster and better than them) to one of facilitating, guiding, or advising with no responsibility for their actions.

Paul had been the CEO of a company for many years. He had guided his company through many challenges, acquisitions, and transformations. He deeply enjoyed the business. When leaving his company, there were many opportunities for him to lead other companies, but he chose to be on the board of a couple of nonprofit organizations and start-up companies. He was excited by all that he was learning about the new businesses, and he respected (mostly) the senior executive teams. As a director on the board of these companies, he was not expected to generate business for them, seek funding sources, or be an expert in their businesses. He was an advisor who would bring executive and leadership perspectives to the CEO and other members of management, and this would help them think more strategically about their businesses as they grew and developed. He was paid for this work, but that didn't really matter to Paul. He was there because he knew that he could make a positive difference.

After a successful banking career, John F. started and manages a program to bring mentors to high school students. His program pairs working adults with aspiring young people to help them think about career opportunities and learn how to be successful in workplace environments. Many of these mentor relationships turn into lasting friendships. He now coaches both the mentors and students, and he has seen significant benefits to both.

Suzanne has become certified as a life coach. She enjoys the engagement with her clients, but the marketing is more challenging than she expected. She keeps exploring ways to find clients and provide her special skills in new, creative ways.

Randy had been a coach all his professional life. His background was described earlier. He has now moved beyond coaching others and works to support the sport through a regional association. He has taken a special interest in reclaiming important historical events, trophies, and memorabilia about the sport. He has connected with a local museum to house a wealth of items. He is working to create "historical memories" of the sport for future generations.

When you seek to become a coach or advisor, you bring experiences to the relationship and can help others learn from your experience, wisdom, and judgment. You provide guidance, but the work does not belong to you. It is vitally important to let the others do the work that is needed, listen, and consider what you may have to say, but it is their responsibility to do what they feel is important. You are not doing the work for them. You are not their boss. You are an advisor, a consultant, a resource that they may or may not use. While they may make mistakes or exercise poor judgments, it is important for them to learn from these experiences.

3) Traveler, Explorer, Adventurer

This is the person who loves to plan and take trips. While you may have a home base of operations, you seek to explore new places, learn their history, and experience their unique cultures and customs. These could be in the United States (or your local country) or in the far reaches of the globe. These could be through expanding the area where you have lived most of your life, extending farther out with each venture.

You love to read books about places you have gone or want to go to. You want to have adventures and experiences. You do the things you love doing in faraway and unusual places. You enjoy meeting new people and making new friends in many parts of the world. You feel a connection with different countries and cultures. You want to see all parts of the world that you've known about but never experienced. You love to tell stories about your travels and may wear souvenirs or proudly display treasures you obtained on these adventures. Fundamentally, you see yourself as a traveler, an explorer, and adventurer, and a wanderer. You may only do this for a few years, but now is the time to do this. This kind of life feeds your soul.

Shannon recently spent more than a month living in Mexico, learning the language, staying with friends, and exploring. She did a similar trip in Thailand and used her rental property as a home base from which she would take extended exploratory trips and stay with the people in their homes. She found a strong connection with the cultures she visited, and it deepened her sense of the world. She did this on a shoestring budget. These people are not your standard tourists, and they want to deeply experience the places they visit.

Betsy says that one thing she really enjoys is planning for her adventure vacations. "I'm a planner and getting ready is as fun for me as doing the trip." Sometimes she travels with friends, her boyfriend, or her children. If her trip takes her near her grandchildren, she always takes a few days to be with them. She keeps herself very healthy by vigorous exercise and participating in sports, and this gives her the stamina and energy to pursue adventure travel.

Karen and Jim sold their home and bought a recreational vehicle. Then, they traveled throughout the United States for more than five years. They went to places they had always wanted to see. They found a community of kindred explorers and frequently met them again at different campgrounds. They stayed for as long as they wanted, and then they moved on to explore new places. They have many stories to share with their friends and family.

There are those who enjoy finding ways to do these things on a limited budget. Regardless of the amount (from super first class to travel pauper), they like to find deals in how they do these adventures. This helps them live within their financial limits and feel a sense of accomplishment when they find a great deal to do something fun and unusual.

Further, we are seeing significant changes in how the travel industry is responding to the increased demands of adventurers. The number of people moving into these activities is significant, as the baby boomers move from work life to new freedoms and have the lust and resources for travel. In many cases, people are taking multiple-generation travel adventures so that parents (grandparents), their children, and their children (grandchildren) can share some of the same adventures. This strengthens family bonds and creates new experiences for all. People are traveling in groups with their college alma maters and professional associations, and these become a source of new friends and can support one's college or profession.

The travel industry has recognized this trend and realizes that individuals at this stage of life offer a significant growth market. According to the World Tourism Organization (WTO), the travel market for people over fifty-five is the fastest-growing segment. A change from typical tourist vacations to experience-based holidays are impacting this industry greatly. This market has a higher demand for quality and sophistication, an increasing awareness of environmental and sustainability issues, and itineraries that are longer and more individually managed. People in the baby boomer generation have more time and financial resources and seek to create stronger experience-based learning adventures than in past generations.[94]

Toby and David have found many low-cost but highly meaningful tour companies. This enables them to travel on a tight budget and take in the world without blowing away their assets. Carl and Sandy have renovated a van to be more suited to living and traveling. They now go on many low-cost adventures and drive around the country to see many hidden corners of the country.

Sam and Sarah like to travel first class to exciting resorts in faraway places. They love to ride horses, play golf, do adventure tours, and drink local wines. They often travel with sponsored groups that are professionally organized and run. They enjoy finding discounts when they can, but they mostly seek and appreciate the experiences.

The fastest-growing segments of the market include genealogical tourism, adventure tourism, multigenerational travel, educational travel, and volunteering travel. Suzanne and John often take genealogy vacations and go to places and learn about the varied lives of their ancestors (especially hers). These all reflect a different sort of traveler than one who merely wants to see tourist sites. These are people who want to be engaged, find meaning in the travel experience, and have the time and financial resources to demand this level of service. There are many ways to live the life of a traveler.

---

[94] "Tourism 2020 Vision," World Tourism Organization, Europe. Vol. 4, ISBN:978-9284403806, UNWTO.

4) Artist/Craftsperson/Author/Musician

This is the person who loves to build things, create things, take things apart and put them back together, and invent and develop new things. You spend a lot of time in your workshop, studio, basement, or garage, at your computer, easel, guitar, or pottery wheel, or behind a camera. You have your special place, your cave, or your creative spot. You could build furniture, create sculptures, or join a band that can make full use of your musical talents. You could be a painter, a drawing artist, or a writer. You want to write that book that is inside of you. The resources available to those who are "pregnant with a book" have grown dramatically, and the cost and effort to publish has fallen dramatically. The popularity and acceptance of self-published books are a testimony to this trend for authors. There are many tools or supplies to support this drive. You could be a musician or actor who loves to perform for others. You could be a gardener or like to dig your hands into natural things and support life—to be viewed, shared, or consumed.

While this is often a solitary task, you may find great joy in sharing your talents with friends and family members. You often exist in your own unique world, and while you may make money doing this, this is usually not your purpose. You have a passion to create, research, develop, and express something important. In your heart, you are an artist. What you do may change the world or give you or someone else a special experience through your creative works.

An executive with a major US corporation, as he was gradually separating from his company, auditioned for a band. It turns out he was a great guitar player, and the band welcomed him. His new agent found opportunities for him to perform in a variety of venues. Richard has fun performing on Friday nights at a local restaurant. He works hard to prepare his playlist, and the customers enjoy the music he provides. For both of them, music has become an important channel for their creative energy.

Anne F. discovered her love of acting when participating in a few plays at her church and as a member of a local ensemble theater group. She took acting classes and developed a resume for acting. She auditions now for community theater and loves being cast in short, fun plays. The big change for her came when she realized that she just enjoyed being on stage and didn't really want a new career. She was doing this for the pure love of the craft. And if she got a lot of applause, as she often did, that was icing on the cake.

Peter N. has rediscovered his creative energy at the pottery wheel. This well-established and successful architect has recently rediscovered something he used to do as a young adult. He loves creating things and building things and then giving them away as gifts. He is finding this is his newfound hobby. Being in his midfifties, he is thinking about his next stage. He wonders if there will be opportunities to do more with this pottery and other pursuits. He's not ready to leave his work, and he simply can't afford to either, but till that day comes, he has discovered something he can take with him into the new stage and will experience the energy and fun that is the foundation of his profession.

One of the important factors for many in this stage is making money from their passions. As indicated above, this may not be the driving force, but it may be necessary given their current or future financial situation. There are resources that can help you develop channels for marketing and selling your work. Websites like etsy.com or artfine.com are sources for selling one's creative products. Regardless of the action, what you really enjoy is being an artist.

5) Sports Enthusiast/Athlete

Sports is a major entertainment industry and impacts many sectors of society. This person loves sports—to watch it, play it, get better at it, and do it with others. Often individuals are interested in many sports and use this time to fill a passion and build deep friendships. Whether the sport is golf, tennis, cycling, jogging, football, baseball, basketball, soccer, or pickleball, these activities create important sources for fun, exercise, and friendships. It can also include hiking, skiing, surfing, and piloting airplanes or gliders for fun.

When many people leave the workplace, they focus on their golf or tennis games. This becomes a source for deep passion, financial investment, and a community of friends. Often to the dismay of their spouses, those who dive deeply into the sport find endless hours are applied to studying the game, watching others play, practicing, developing skills, and playing the game. They have special equipment, clothing, display cases for trophies or mementoes, and more. They may seek a home near a golf course or join clubs and programs to improve their games. They participate in tournaments and local competitions to feed their passion for the game. Avid hikers may live near hiking trails, and tennis players may live near courts. People move their bases of operations to be near the things they love or places where the weather is better suited to their sport.

With advances in technology, many people will be able to keep participating in their chosen sport well into their later years of life. They have hips, shoulders and knees replaced so they can continue to enjoy life and the sports that provide great meaning to them. Jack, at age ninety-three, had a knee replaced so that he could continue with his tennis game. He also hit a hole in one on the golf course at age ninety-four and received a trophy and much acclaim by his community of friends.

As mentioned earlier, Dick is a cyclist. In addition to local rides, he participates in challenging trips, like in Yellowstone Park, around the Grand Canyon, and in trips globally. He has connected to a large group of individuals that share his enthusiasm, and he makes sure he has the best equipment he can afford. This interest keeps him healthy while providing great satisfaction from completing amazing trips.

Soon after Mary's husband died, she discovered how much she loved being outdoors. The years of caring for her husband had taken a toll on her spirit. She rediscovered this spirit as she got into hiking, cycling, skiing, and jogging. She has improved her personal health, found new adventures, and has found a channel to invest her boundless energy. She has a new life, and it involves being active, outside, and engaging with friends and her grandchildren.

You may invest in a personal trainer or coach to assist you in improving your abilities, which enhances your enjoyment and meaning of the game. This lifestyle can create a strong sense of connection with others who share your passions. For almost every sport or activity imaginable, there is likely a large group of people with whom you can connect. You can build a strong community of people with shared passions, and you can get healthier through regular exercise at the same time. You have much in common and can engage in a variety of discussions about people and players, techniques, the latest equipment, games, sporting events, and the history of the sport. It is all very exciting and a source of great enjoyment and satisfaction, especially if you play well!

6) Volunteer/Social Activist/One Who Gives Back

The volunteer is that special person who pursues opportunities to give back, create, or strengthen mission-driven organizations. You seek to make a strong, positive difference in the lives of others and the world. You may have done this kind of work in small chunks of time while working and raising children, but now you can be more purposeful and more fully engaged.

The types of activities are wide-ranging. Some will be deeply involved in their churches, religious organizations, or local community organizations. Some will be involved in special issue-focused causes such as homelessness, food shelters, social justice, or immigration. Some will be involved in foreign service programs and causes like the Peace Corps, the Clinton Foundation, Oxfam America, the Gates Foundation, or similar organizations that address global, regional, or local issues. Some will become global volunteers, investing their time in communities far from home. They are making a difference in the lives of people in a personal way. Some will be involved in coaching children or helping out students with special needs. Some people will be involved in helping nonprofit organizations improve themselves through organizations like Encore.org, SCORE (Service Corps of Retired Executives—www.score. org) or Habitat for Humanity (www.Habitat.org). Some organizations will focus on disaster relief (Red Cross, Catholic Charities, Unitarian Universalist Service Committee), and others address health, water, or other basic human services. There are many programs available and in great need of the talents of experienced people. There are websites that will match your interests with those in need. Try Volunteer Match (www.volunteermatch.com) or Go Abroad (www.goabroad.com). Many organizations offer ways you can contribute your time, talents, and treasures (money).

Since Anne F. loves working with children, it was a natural move to enter the classroom as a volunteer teacher's assistant to provide support to teachers and spend time with kids she has grown to love. She keeps her time limited, and the work provides enormous satisfaction to her and the teachers she supports.

With a friend, Bill founded a nonprofit organization to help rehabilitate and redirect men who are headed to prison. He is applying his years as both an attorney and judge, where he saw the impact of justice system firsthand, to train, counsel, and change the lives of men who have committed serious crimes before they become trapped in the prison life. This program is modeled after a similar program for women who have been convicted of crimes. Although it is in its initial stages, it has already had a significant impact on his community. There are many people who find a special niche where they can make a true difference and bring expertise, passion, and connections to help support these mission-driven organizations.

After Fred retired, he took the opportunity to become much more active in social justice and other work through his church. Since leaving a major technology firm, he has taken on the issue of political corruption due to virtually unlimited campaign funding from corporations and wealthy individuals. He has started a group that has gained a great deal of support and is building connections with other organizations in the US. He is fully applying his organizational, leadership, and mission-driven abilities to address the corruption being created by money in politics.

Lori initially began volunteering for a program called Age-in-Place.[95] She soon became the chairperson of the organization in the town where she and her husband have a summer home. Age-in-Place is a program that provides all the services and amenities people seek in an assisted-living facility—but it is provided directly in one's home. This program is built around communities and enables the members to receive services, participate in organized social events, and find companionship so that they are not alone as they age. This is a national network and

---

[95]   www.AgeinPlace.com.

is becoming an important contributor to people who want to live in their local communities. Lori is excited about growing, supporting, and assisting the staff in the development of this program within her adopted community.

Some will try one or more of these alternatives and find that they really are not meaningful. This was an important lesson for Toby. She started working as a volunteer helping disadvantaged people budget and manage their finances. While this was important to some, Toby soon found that neither she nor her clients were gaining much benefit. She felt she should continue because if one did not sacrifice in doing volunteer work, it wouldn't count. But then she realized that other volunteer activities were bringing great joy to her and value to the organization. She stopped her counseling work and focused on where she was making a difference. This was an important insight. Volunteering should create value, engagement, and benefit to all involved.

Participating in programs like those cited above often provides individuals with significant opportunities to make important contributions. The world has many needs, and many organizations are seeking to fulfill those needs. As you have more time, there are many organizations that can use your talents. Often, the hard part is saying no to a program that could benefit from your talents and finding the balance between needed opportunities and how you use your time and talents. When people move away from their employers, they often find they have lost important social connections and communities. The right mission-driven organizations can fill this important gap and replace those things you once had in the workplace.

7) Lifelong Learner/Perpetual Student

This person is the perpetual student. You love to learn and engage in educational experiences. The important difference is that you don't worry about exams, class credits, or a major unless you are seeking a special degree. You can take courses, participate in field studies (domestic and foreign), engage in projects and discussion groups, and attend powerful lectures. You are a lover of learning, and you continually seek ways to learn more about a specific subject or a broad range of studies.

Those who pursue this lifestyle may live close to an academic center or university. They participate in campus activities and may be one of those seniors who often stand out in a young person's world. Fortunately, the trend is clearly moving in their direction, and soon they will no longer be one of the few. Many universities are reaching out to this new marketplace and developing programs that appeal to this market of learners. There are programs at colleges and universities. There are many online programs available, and many are offered by universities and community centers in towns and cities. Some of them include edX.org, Coursera.org, Udemy.com, and MOOC-list.com.

Toby has completed more than forty online courses in the past few years, and as she digs into different subjects, her thirst for learning more about a subject grows. She says she could spend hours doing this and realizes there is so much more to learn and experience.

Jeff has taken his interest in comparative religions to a new level. He is taking courses at a major university and has expressed some interest in gaining a degree. He is highly engaged in the class discussions, reading the materials, and exploring different religions' ceremonies. While he doesn't really enjoy writing the papers, they do give him an opportunity to further develop his thoughts and ideas. Grades are of little interest, but he is doing well. He doesn't know where this will lead. For Jeff, the joy of learning something more deeply than he did when he was in college is where he is finding value.

Fran has taken her love of learning to the next level. For years, she has been interested in the impact of World War I on world history. She wanted an outlet for this interest and an opportunity to learn even more. She developed a course and is teaching at the American University's Osher Lifelong Learning Institute. Similar programs exist at other universities, and they provide opportunities for people like Fran to attend or lead these programs and expand their love of learning. She has found that one learns even more when one is engaged in teaching the subject to others.

The costs for these programs are evolving as more programs become available. Many are being promoted at low or minimal cost through a variety of websites (such as seniorcitizenguideforcollege.com). There may be scholarships, waivers, or organizations that financially support senior learners and help them participate in these programs. Much is evolving with the programs, and research that is local and global may be worth the effort to identify and try out. The pursuit of learning enriches one's life and helps enrich one's life in multiple dimensions. There is so much out there that is ready to be learned.

8) Dilettante/Dabbler/Improvisational Specialist

This is the continually curious person. You seek to learn, experience, and do things as they come. You pursue interests with no particular objective or mission. You use this time to enjoy and experience many different things. You may wake up each day and determine what you want to do that day. Then, at the end of the day, you look back and feel fulfilled that you did something interesting. At times, you don't feel that much has been done that day. You don't seek achievements. You have successfully left this motivation behind. You may become engaged in a project that can take days, weeks, or months, but it will end, and then you can be on to the next thing. Each day is unique, different, and not driven by goals.

The Greek philosopher Epicurus believed that the happiest life is one that is free from self-imposed demands of commerce and politics.[96] When we get to this stage, then the best pursuits are to reflect on the pleasures of life, using time to be with friends and fill life with leisurely pleasures. He encourages people to savor the privilege of having lived this long, and then when it is your time, you transcend to somewhere else. He says this is the time to adjust your wants to your abilities and simplify your life and activities to the most basic ones that bring you pleasure and joy.

You may take care of the infrastructure of life for your family or for yourself, but mostly you're pursuing a wide variety of interests. You take classes for a while in philosophy, piano, or other areas. You take up activities or explore subjects because you are curious. You may become an enthusiast or an aficionado about specific things. You may see yourself as a dilettante and will address life as it comes. You value

---

[96]   Klein, Daniel, *Travels with Epicurus*, Penguin Books, New York, 2012.

your freedom, flexibility, and openness to new adventures without commitments.

Phil L. is involved in many things. For several hours per week, he becomes a companion to veterans who live in nursing homes and have little family. He becomes a friend to them and loves to hear and share their stories. He also works at times with Habitat for Humanity, and he helps renovate or build homes for low-wage people. He enjoys the camaraderie of his workmates and learning new skills in the process. He sees the excitement and joy on the faces of the people who will be living in their new homes. He occasionally does redecorating or repair/maintenance work for friends. Some are local, and others are distant. After their work for the day, he enjoys a beer and good conversation. His life is full of pursuits, but he couldn't tell you what he was going to be doing the next day or next week.

Bev, after a very successful career, is interested in many things. She loves to play bridge and being involved with a meaningful group of women in a book group. While she has lots of projects, she is pleased that there are no restraints on her time. She does what she wants when she does it. She exercises on most days and enjoys her time at the gym. She walks with friends several times per week and keeps in touch with friends through morning coffees and afternoon teas. She is active in several volunteer organizations associated with her church and takes leadership roles when necessary. She plans adventure vacations for herself, her husband, their children, and their spouses. She loves her family and goes to visit them periodically. While she sometime worries that she is not more purpose driven, she finds that her greatest meaning (and joy) comes from engaging with others about their lives, their activities, and their interests. She feels her life is full of love and fun activities. She simply likes it that way.

Dean also sees himself as a curious person who is interested in many things. He has picked up playing the piano again and is improving his skills; the piano was an instrument he loved earlier in his life. He has become an excellent cook and has a bountiful garden. He enjoys taking courses in philosophy and literature and listens to long stretches of classical music. His days are full of enrichment and interest. While he struggles with the sense at times that he is not accomplishing anything, he finds this time of life suited perfectly to doing the things he always wanted to do. Many days are full of learning and experiences, but he realizes that these all depend on his own self-motivation. He has realized that he is the one who is fully responsible for how he spends this time.

This is the person who has given themselves permission to go and do and be what they want. Their meaning comes from the wide variety of things they do and the spontaneity that comes with the dilettante's lifestyle.

9) Grandparent/Primary Resource Center

This is the person whose family responsibilities have increased, and they enjoy creating a family and nurturing others. There was a time when your children were the center of your activities and life. Now, the kids have grown and started their own families. There was a time when you had relatively little engagement in their lives, but as they have children, careers, and possibly health issues, you are called back into service.

Jerry thought he could live anywhere in the world and was exploring living in less expensive countries. When his daughter gave birth to his first grandchild, he lost his interest in living somewhere else. He wanted to be close to this family and be a strong presence in the lives of his grandchildren. Phil B., as discussed earlier, had a similar experience.

In some communities, people are doing this kind of work for others who are not formally related. They do this because at their core, they just love being with, nurturing, and loving children. For these people, the ancient African proverb is very real: "It takes a village to raise a child." You become a resource for others in the neighborhood or community. In some families, the grandparents won't be seen except on special occasions or for periodic visits, or schedule weekly FaceTime or video-chat calls, and others will be the primary resource and backup to their children and grandchildren. You may become a Big Sister or a Big Brother and take on the role of guiding and supporting a child who does not have a nurturing parent relationship.[97] It is important to remember that the children are in their own stages of life, which is different than

---

[97]   Big Brother Big Sister of America: www.bbbs.org.

yours, and they need the space and freedom to pursue the lifestyle suited to those stages. And through this time, your heart grows bigger as you share it with others.

10) Seeker of Enlightenment and Personal Growth

Buddhism teaches us that the pathway to enlightenment is through mindfulness, awareness of the present moment, and in all ways to be fully here now. You are the person who is focused on reflection, purposeful examination of yourself, seeking to experience the spiritual presence in all things, and seeing the world through a different set of lenses. Your mission is to experience moments of enlightenment that engage you in a more thoughtful and deeper exploration about the purpose of life and the mysteries of the spirit. Each spiritual path— whether it be Taoist, Jewish, Buddhist, Hindu, Christian, Unitarian Universalism, or Mother Nature—leads to enlightenment and salvation in its own way. You are on a quest for awakening, understanding, and spirituality. Your journey leads to a sense of calmness and acceptance that is not found in the other lifestyles. The pathway is different for each person, but there are guideposts that can lead you along their way. Your passion is to find them and follow them.

Jim once worked for a major global consulting firm, held several exciting executive positions, and was a Unitarian Universalist minister. As he entered this next stage, he has grown into a seeker. Over the years he has traveled to India, Ecuador, and Thailand and walked in the steps of Buddha, studied with Sufis, Taoists, Hindus, Transcendentalists, and Jewish and Christian spiritual teachers. He experienced an opening to his life that brought great insights and a spiritual awakening. He tells of how this has brought him a sense of unity, clarity, and interconnectedness to all beings. He found a purpose and a calling. He is sharing these experiences and this presence through his writings and working with groups of other individuals on a similar quest to learn and enrich themselves spiritually.[98]

---

[98]   Sherblom, Jim Rev. Dr., *Spiritual Audacity*, Wise Ink Creative Publishing, Minneapolis, MN, 2018.

So, this could be a time to focus on those things which give you meaning, spirituality, personal growth, and insights. Because we have spent most of our lives seeking, driving, and achieving, reorienting our lives to be focused on the here and now can be quite challenging. This is mindfulness, this is being with Buddha, and this is exploring the Hindu teachings, Christian gospel, Jewish Torah, Muslim Quran (Koran), transcendentalism, or diving into many religions that offer insights into life's mysteries. The mission of individuals pursuing this lifestyle is one of seeking a deep understanding of life's purpose and the universality and humanity of all existence with a deep sense of their own presence. Their journey is both deep inside and well beyond the achievement-oriented society.

Redefining Who You Are

There are many other pathways one may choose. While these summaries describe many, you may know someone who is doing something very different—or you may have ideas that are different. You should explore what these alternatives hold for you. Which ones are particularly interesting to you? Why are they appealing? Is this something you would like to do as you enter this next stage? Is this something that you would like to do at some other point in the future? What conditions would make this the right time for them? The important message is to think creatively, think broadly, and remember that this is your time for your life—and there is no one telling you what you should do.

One of the greatest opportunities that this stage of life provides is that you can pursue a mix of activities and adventures that fulfill you. Then, several years later, you can change them. You can feel that you've done what you wanted and reconfigure your lifestyle into a new pattern. These are the mini stages discussed earlier. There are few obligations that hold you back. This is a time to experiment with different things, see what creates the passion described earlier, and discover what you would like to see yourself doing.

How you structure and fill your time, what you do with your interests and passions, and how these actions support a responsible and healthy life create the platform for your life in this next stage. These actions will define your identity and help you describe yourself to others. And your lifestyle can change and flow with new interests and new passions during this stage. There will be a time when you won't have the flexibility or capabilities to do the things available to you during this stage. As is often asked in this book, if not now, when? The lifestyle choices are yours to make. You have the responsibility to choose wisely. You also can make mistakes, learn from them, recover, and redirect your talents in different directions. What is more important than building an identity and lifestyle that you can enjoy, knowing you have a plan that provides you the experiences that bring life to life. So, in the words of Captain Jean-Luc Picard of *Star Trek: Next Generation*, "Make it so."

Chapter 9
Developing Your Master Plan

Do not go where the path may lead, go instead
where there is no path and leave a trail.
—Ralph Waldo Emerson

Throughout this book, you have read summaries of research studies, stories of people living their next stages, and guides to help you understand your current situation. In this chapter, we're going to develop a Master Plan by focusing on actions you can take in the five areas covered in the previous chapters: time, finances, relationships, health, and identity/lifestyle. These are the pillars for determining your direction as you enter and live your Reinventing Adulthood stage. We will work through a series of exercises, checklists, and worksheets that will help you prepare your Master Plan. You may use the pages in this book or use separate paper, worksheets, or a notebook to address the questions presented below. You may do this now or when you're ready to develop a plan. This is your plan, and this is for you. Let's get started.

Question 1: What do you want to do with your time?

An important theme throughout this book is how to use your time wisely. You are closer to the end of life than the beginning. We have continually addressed the unique nature of this time in life. Chapter 4 examined the factors to consider in using this time well. You may no longer have responsibility for a job, children to raise, or other obligations that are not of your choosing. This is a time to determine what you want to do that is different from what you have done in the past and identify those things that will give you meaning, purpose, and fulfillment. So, one day, you will look back on this life and feel that it was good and worthwhile.

The first step in building your Master Plan is to determine how you want to use your time so that it provides the greatest value to you. In chapter 4, we started by identifying where and when you were in your zone. This is a place where you feel fully engaged and energized by what you are doing. Perhaps in these areas, you will find how to best spend your time during this next stage. After all, your obligation is only to you and perhaps other commitments you have to your family and friends.

In chapter 4, I asked you to brainstorm a list of times when you were in your zone or truly enjoying what you were doing. Go back and look at this list. By now, you probably have reflected on these times. As you begin building your Master Plan, let's look at these times again with greater insight about what you find engaging and energizing. Complete the tasks presented below in the box and reflect on what they mean.

Identify 3 to 5 activities that you love doing, feel totally engaged and energized by them, and you are fully "in your zone."

As you look over these experiences, you can probably see patterns or similarities between them. What were the feelings that were in common? What were the actions that were in common? In chapter 4, we translated these themes into guideposts. Go back and look at them and their definitions. Once you have done this, use the worksheet below to check the one or ones that have been most important to you—and then identify the ones you want to continue using to guide your pathway during the next stage of your life.

Review the guideposts listed below (the descriptions are shown in chapter 4). Identify which ones reflect the activities you do when you are fully engaged and energized (i.e., "in your zone"). Describe what it is about the guidepost that creates this feeling in you. Then, rate them (High, Medium, or Low) for how important they are to you.

☐ Achievement

☐ Leadership

☐ Helping Others

☐   **Relationships and Connections with Others**

☐   **Personal Creativity and Growth**

☐   **Making the World a Better Place**

☐   **Other:** _____

Describe this:

In this next step, we will review and summarize your unique abilities. There were many tools referenced in chapter 4. Hopefully you utilized one or several of them to gain a deeper and clearer understanding of the unique abilities you bring to each situation. Like the guideposts, knowing your particular strengths will help you make better decisions about what you want to be doing in this next stage. You want to use those talents where you can be most effective and develop new ones that build on these core strengths. You know you have certain talents—even though you may be humble about expressing them. This task is for you to define and learn more about yourself. Use some of the tools and references that were described in chapter 4. They can be very helpful.

What are the unique abilities that enable you to accomplish or perform the things you do well?

This brings us to the task of identifying those things you want to do during this stage of your life. The core message here is to identify the things that give you a sense of purpose and support the things that you want to do in this next stage. Remember, happiness comes from meaning, but meaning seldom comes from happiness. Your task is to answer the questions below. These are activities that start with things you have not yet done in your life, and you will identify the things you want to do more of, the things you have to do, and the things you want to do less of. It ends with identifying the things you no longer want to spend time doing. Remember to build on your talents and unique abilities—unless you really want to learn to do something very different. Examine your brainstormed list of experiences and identify what you want to do with this special time in your life.

The key questions for you to address are:

1. What are those things you've always wanted to do but have never done them or done them to your desired level? What are those things you want to start doing?

2. What are those things you want to do more of and get very good at?

3. What are those things you feel obligated to keep doing because of a commitment or responsibility that you have for something or someone?

4. What do you want to do less of or reduce doing?

5. What do you want to stop doing? It may take a little time, but you want to eliminate this from your activities?

From these lists of actions and activities, <u>identify the 5 most important to you.</u> Mark them above or list them below.. Briefly describe why they are important to you in this Next Stage of your life.

Question 2: Will you have enough money?

This next set of questions and answers has an important bearing on whether you will be able to do those things you just identified in the previous section. It is very important to assess your income and expenses and develop a financial plan and process for managing your expenses, assets, and income so that you can live the life you wish within your available resources or in the most optimal manner.

As you examine the areas of the financial plan presented in chapter 5, how much of this information do you have readily available? Have you examined it carefully? To what extent have you discussed this with your spouse or life partner? Are you two in full agreement? Are there others who should be included in your financial planning because of their relationship to you? Will anyone else be significantly impacted by your assumptions, projections, and actions in these areas?

Below are a series of worksheets that you may use to collect and summarize your financial information. This work will not replace the work of a good financial planner, but it may help you in preparing for and understanding what kind of advisor you will need. It may help you have thoughtful and meaningful discussions with your significant other.

We will start with your expenses and then examine your sources of income. Once you compare them, your actions may lead you to do one or both differently. Your expense projections should include the costs you may incur pursuing the wants you defined in the previous section over time. Below is a list of possible expenses that are categorized as fixed, semi-fixed, and variable (see chapter 5 if you need an explanation of these). Some of these expenses are paid annually, and some are paid monthly.

For purposes of planning, you should convert all the monthly expenses into annual numbers. This will be helpful when comparing this to your income projections. However, cash flow is important, and you will obviously need to prepare for any major annual expenses by having cash available. You may want to put this information on a separate sheet and provide the summary on this page or a similar document that you can work with.

Your Expense Budget				
Expense Items:	**Monthly**		**Annual**	
Fixed Expenses:				
Mortgage	$	-	$	-
Other debt: car loan, credit cards, etc.	$	-	$	-
Utilities: heat, electricity, water, cable, internet	$	-	$	-
Taxes: Auto excise, Property, and other taxes	$	-	$	-
Medical expenses and prescriptions	$	-	$	-
Insurance: Life, health, home, auto, long-term care	$	-	$	-
Other fixed expenses	$	-	$	-
Total Fixed Expenses:	*S*	-	*S*	-
Semi-Fixed Expenses:				
Groceries	$	-	$	-
Supplies and home maintenance	$	-	$	-
Auto expenses: gas, service	$	-	$	-
Club membership(s)	$	-	$	-
Gifts: Birthdays, Weddings and Christmas (other)	$	-	$	-
Other semi-variable expenses	$	-	$	-
Total Semi-Variable Expenses:	*S*	-	*S*	-
Variable Expenses:				
Dinners Out	$	-	$	-
Entertainment	$	-	$	-
Contributions to church and charities	$	-	$	-
Travel	$	-	$	-
Person 1's general expenses	$	-	$	-
Person 2's general expenses	$	-	$	-
Other variable expenses	$	-	$	-
Total Variable Expenses:	*S*	-	*S*	-
Total Expenses:	*S*	-	*S*	-

Other Planned Major Expenses:	$	-	$	-
(Weddings, Car or Home Purchase, Educational	When are they likely to occur?			

How confident are you in these numbers? What do you see changing as you transition from working full-time to living in this next stage of life? How might these numbers change over the next five years, ten years, or twenty years? Note if there will be any particular major expenditures that are likely to occur and when you think they might happen. What are your projections for inflation and it's impact on your expenses? This will be discussed below. It is important to understand what you may likely face in all expenditures and how these are likely to change over time.

Now let's examine your sources for income. You need to consider the sources of income after you have completed your working career and how might this amount of earned income will change as you enter this next stage of your life. We assume that you will somehow not be working as you did when you were in the Pinnacle Adulthood stage of your career.

Just as you may have done when examining expenses, you may want to put this information on a separate sheet. Then provide a summary or total of each source on the worksheet below or a similar form that works for you.

Your Income Sources		
Income Sources:	**Asset Value**	**Annual Amount**
Earned Income:		
Person 1		$ -
Person 2		$ -
Total		$ -
Secured Income:		
Social Security: Person 1		$ -
Pension: Person 1		$ -
Social Security: Person 2		
Pension: Person 2		$ -
Total		$ -
Other Income:		
Rental properties		$ -
Other income sources		$ -
Total		$ -
Current Total Assets		
Secondary residence	$ -	
Other real estate properties	$ -	
Invested assets - in retirement accounts	$ -	
Invested assets - in taxable accounts	$ -	
Savings (held in cash or CD's)	$	
Other assets	$ -	
Total Assets	$ -	
Note: Your primary residence should not be included unless you are going to use it as as source for investment income.		
Withdrawal from invested assets:		
4% withdrawal rate		$ -
5% withdrawal rate		$ -
CoRI withdrawal rate		$ -
Average of 3 alternatives withdrawal rates		$ -
Total projected income		$ -
Less provisions for State & Federal income taxes		$ -
Net after tax income		$ -
Other sources of income and projected timing		
1		$ -
2		$ -
3		$ -

As was asked about your expenses, how much confidence do you have in these numbers? If you don't know your tax liability at this time, you can estimate a general projection by visiting several websites. A particularly useful one can be found at: www.calcxml.com/do/federal-income-tax-calculator?skn=73. Remember, under current Social Security tax law and depending on your overall income, only 85 percent of your projected Social Security income is treated as ordinary income. The other 15 percent comes to you tax-free! Be aware, however, that this might change. Again, consult your financial advisor about your likely tax obligations given your different sources of income.

You need to pull these numbers together and examine the results. You may use the worksheet below. What do the results show you about your estimates? How confident are you in the numbers you provided? What conclusions can you draw about your current financial situation?

Putting the Numbers Together	Annual	Comments:
Total Projected Income	$ -	
Provisions for State & Federal income taxes	$ -	
Net Income after Taxes	$ -	
Total Projected Annual Expenses		
Fixed	$ -	
Semi-Variable	$ -	
Variable	$ -	
Total Projected Expenses	$ -	
Difference Between Income and Expenses	$ -	
Percent Difference (Divide total expenses by total income, and then subtract "1". This will give you a percent.) Enter that number here:	%	

This is only a one-year snapshot about where you are. The task you have is to work with a financial planner and project how this is likely to change in the future. At several points, you will need to make assumptions. You may need to establish a few in order to make a reasonable projection of how your financial condition may change over time.

Factors That May Impact Your Financial Condition

What is your assumption about increases in the cost of living? Which items are likely to change with the prevailing rate of inflation? Which expenses or income will be impacted by the general economy?

What is your assumption about how your investments will grow over time? What is your asset allocation's mix between equity investments, bonds, and fixed income or secured income? How might the overall investment performance impact your total invested assets?

How might your tax rate change as your income changes in terms of the overall amount or the sources of that income (ordinary income, capital gains income, nontaxable income, etc.).

Finally, to what extent have you documented where your funds are located, banks or financial institutions, account numbers, usernames and passwords, wills, estate documents, and any contractual obligations? One person interviewed for this book had all this information in a binder/notebook, and everyone in her family knew where to find this document if something were to happen to her. This is an excellent idea, especially for those who are not by nature particularly well organized. This would be an important task to do to support your Master Plan.

Conclusions and Actions for Your Financial Plan

As you have examined the key elements of your financial conditions and discussed them with your spouse or life partner and a thoughtful financial planner, where do you come out on the financial conditions? Here is a list of the ratings. The definitions are shown in chapter 5. Check the one that describes where you are and then add any comments or observations about this assessment.

___ Level 1: Significant Deficit

_____

_____

___ Level 2: Moderate Deficit

_____

_____

___ Level 3: Relative Balance

_____

_____

___ Level 4: Moderate Surplus

_____

_____

____ **Level 5: Significant Surplus**

_____

_____

Based on your answers to these questions, you should have a better perspective of what you know, what you don't know, and how you see your overall financial future.

Question 3: Who do you want to live with?

Chapter 6 addresses this question, and we realize that this is not really about a single relationship. It is about the nature of your relationships with others, your community, and your level of connections with them. In this guide, you should examine who they are, how important they are to you, and what you want to change for the future. Hopefully, you did the Concentric Circles exercise in chapter 6 (if not, go back and do this now) and have had an opportunity to reflect on how close or far people are to you. The following worksheet should help provide an assessment and identify what you want to do that changes, reinforces, develops, and maximizes some of these relationships. There are clear and consistent findings from the research on health and longevity; the type and quality of relationships you have can have a major impact on your life and well-being.

Answer the questions below regarding your relationships on the worksheet that follows. The questions and a brief discussion of the intent of the question should help you focus on where and what needs to change.

1) Who are they?

List the names of people who are important to you or who should be considered as you assess your community of relationships. Put one name on each line or box on the worksheet below. They may vary widely, but it is important to identify who specifically you are thinking about as you do this task. This worksheet limits you to seven, but you can add more or use less, depending on who is important to you.

2) What is your relationship with them?

Briefly identify the type of relationship you have with each person on your list. Use the types of relationships that were described in chapter 6:

- core/life partner
- family or family-like
- close friend
- community
- acquaintance

3) How important are they?

Indicate how important these people are to you now. You may use a four-level scale: (1) critical (2) important (3) moderate (4) minor. In many ways, they are on this list because they have some degree of importance to you and to how you see your relationships.

4) What do you want to change or reinforce in this relationship?

This is perhaps the most important question on the worksheet. Describe what you want to change or continue and reinforce. Consider what this means for how you want this relationship to change—and consider whether the other person wants this too. Reflect on why this is important to you and what you can do to facilitate this level of change in your relationship. It is okay to say the relationship is fine and working well. In this case, determine what you will do to support and reinforce your connections.

When you have finished this worksheet, review how you feel about your collection of relationships. Are they as you want—or do you need to make some important changes? As you look at the changes emerging in your life, to what extent are these relationships likely to change? How do you feel about that? Do you need to make any special efforts to address the potential impact of these changes?

Who are they?	What is your relationship with them?	How important are they to you?	What do you want to change or reinforce?

Overall, how do you feel about your pattern of relationships and what changes are needed?

Question 4: How do you stay healthy?

As you know, without your health, many other things you want to do may be limited. Your health is like the foundation for your Next Stage. By doing certain things—many of them are simple but very important—you will likely be able to extend both your life and the quality of your life. Here are some things to keep in mind as you examine your health and develop ways to improve your health and healthy habits.

To what extent do you have healthy habits? Below is a list of twenty conditions or habits that the research presented in chapter 7 correlates highly with healthy people. Let's look at how you compare to these actions. For each item below, select the level that best describes how much you do these things or how well they describe your physical condition and practices. Be honest with yourself; you are the only one who should care strongly about the results. Use the following scale:

1: rarely
2: seldom
3: sometimes
4: often
5: frequently

Rating	How often do these conditions or practices exist for you?
	Keep your overall cholesterol under 180 with LDL under 100 and HDL over 40.
	Retain blood pressure that is usually below 130 over 80
	Keep your Body Mass Index (BMI) between 18.6 – 24.8
	Achieve your desired cardio-heart rate through active exercises at least 5 times per week
	Do stretching exercise for 15 – 20 minutes daily
	Have a program for weightlifting that you use 3 times per week
	Work on reinforcing your balance by standing on one leg regularly or other patterns to improve your balance

	Integrate exercise activities into your daily routine (e.g., walking a lot, using stairs, playing active games, etc.)
	Eat an average of 7 - 10 servings of fruits and vegetables per day
	Eat whole grain bread, whole grain cereals or pasta, instead of foods made with white flour
	Use monounsaturated fats such as canola oil or olive oil
	Enjoy fatty fish (such as mackerel, trout, tuna and salmon) at least twice per week
	Limit dairy products (e.g., milk, cheese or ice cream) to 1% or fat-free
	Limit red meat to less than 2 or 3 times per month (keep it lean, avoid sausage and bacon or other high-fat meats)
	Drink at least 5 glasses of water per day
	Do something that reduces your stress, increases your calmness, and mindfulness
	Take the appropriate vitamins or special dietary supplements
	Engage in activities that enhance your memory, mental agility, and alertness
	Get regular full nights sleep (at least 7 hours per night)
	Do at least one thing that is special for you that is taking care of yourself

After you have completed your ratings of these healthy habits, let's look at what this might mean for you. Add up all the ratings and calculate a total score. Enter it below:

Total Score:_____

If you scored *less than fifty,* you have many changes to make to improve or sustain your health. You indicated that you do many of these healthy habits rarely or seldom. Identify the ones that are most important to you and start taking action now. Circle the ones that you will start paying more attention to. Your life may depend on it.

If you scored *between fifty and eighty,* then you have some good habits in place, but a few clearly need attention. Which are the ones that are most important to you in the short term and the long term? See if you can expand your attention to those areas that need greater emphasis in your life. You will appreciate it even more over time. Circle the ones that you will pay more attention to and improve doing.

If you scored *above eighty,* then you are doing many good things that will benefit you for the rest of your life. While you may face challenges, you are clearly building a strong foundation of healthy habits that should enable you to do many things for the future. You no doubt identified some things that you would want to be better at. Use this time to make refinements in how you retain and promote your health. Encourage and help others who need what you have. Circle the ones that are the most important to you—and this can be a guide for you in the future.

What do you see in these scores? Where are you the strongest? Where do you need to make important adjustments? While each person is different and has unique strengths and limitations, healthy habits form a foundation for what you do that will strengthen your health and abilities.

On the worksheet below, make some notes on what you will do to improve or sustain your health:

	Keep doing what I'm doing now	Start doing or do more of going forward	Stop doing or do less of going forward
Eating Habits			
Exercise Routine			
Something for Myself			

Question 5: Who are you going to be?

One way to identify your image of yourself and the lifestyle you want to live is to look at what others do. In chapter 8, there was a list of ten approaches to life that people in this next stage are pursuing. Go back now and reread each of these and determine which ones resonate with you. You may find several of them of great interest. Some of them may be what you want to start doing as you enter this stage, and others may develop for you over time if there is continued interest in the future. Which ones, as you think about doing them, give you engagement, energy, and excitement? There should be some that are of little to no interest to you.

Now based on your review of these descriptions in chapter 8, indicate below how important each style is (or will be) to you and why. You may consider a few as very important for the next one to three years or three to five years, and others will be important later. Express the importance as a percentage, and then as a total, which should equal 100 percent. Then, briefly describe why the ones you selected are important to you. What are the things that bring out the desired feelings in you?

When you look at what you've indicated as the portfolio of your alternative lifestyle or image of you—and the reasons—your responses may help you determine how to lead your life going forward. Think carefully and answer this question from the voices that are deep inside of you.

Identity, Model, or Life Style	Percent Importance	Why is this important to you?
1. Working Professional		
2. Advisor, Mentor, Guide or Coach		
3. Traveler, Explorer, Adventurer		
4. Artist, Craftsperson, Author, Musician		
5. Sports Enthusiasts, Athlete		
6. Volunteer, Social Activist, One-Who-Gives-Back		
7. Life-long Learner, Perpetual Student		
8. Dilettante, Dabbler, Improvisional Specialist		
9. Grandparent, Primary Resource Center		
10. Seeker of Enlightenment and Personal Growth		

Total = 100%

Your Master Plan

Now is the time to pull all these assessments, action items, to-do lists, and ideas together into a plan that will provide you with direction and confidence. Remember, plans often need to be adjusted, improved, and modified as conditions change. This will be your Master Plan, and no one needs to approve it. You are the one responsible for its development and implementation. This is for your life and your time. You should review this with others to test and get feedback, but you are still in control of and responsible for implementing this plan.

This plan should provide you with a roadmap for charting your course through the next stage of your life. It should be broad enough to provide you with a way to integrate all the areas presented in this book—your talents and passions, your financial conditions, your relationships, ways to remain healthy, and your concept of who you are. It should be action oriented and provide you with a mechanism to motivate you to take action and monitor how you are doing.

It is time to set some priorities and make commitments to yourself. You define what success is and what assistance you will need from others. If you are unsure about what you want to do, that is okay. You are among friends. Use this exercise to identify an area or two where you want to experiment. Try it, see if it works or not, and then modify your plan based on what you've learned or experienced.

Antoine de Saint-Exupery, a French writer, poet, aristocrat, and pioneering aviator in the early twentieth century, said, "A goal without a plan is just a wish." While a wish is nice, it is not likely to guide you to create the life you want.

The following items define the process for developing your Master Plan. Use the worksheets to record your answers, notes, and ideas. This is a special time for you to develop a Master Plan—thoughtfully, personally, and meaningfully—to help you transition to this next stage of your life.

Define the timeframe for your Master Plan: one year, two years, three years, five years, ten years, or more. Enter your time frame below:

_____ years

What do you want to do in each area? Review the work you've done in each of the five areas and identify what you want to do in each area. You will see a box for each of the five areas developed in this book. Summarize what you ultimately want to do in each area. It could be to develop something, try something, research something, learn more about something, define something, or even do less as part of your next stage. When completed, put a star or check next to the three most important areas for actions.

Category:	"I want to …."	Most Important
Your time, interests and talents		
Financial situation or conditions		
Your relationships		
Your healthy habits		
Your identity and lifestyle		

We are going to develop three primary pathways for your life's next stage. Review the primary wants you selected and translate them into three pathways for your life's next stage. A pathway is something you will pursue, a project or mission that will be a primary focus for you over the time period you selected: one to three years, five years, ten years, or longer.

The pathways may be discrete (i.e., each one stands alone) or interdependent (i.e., one builds on or toward one of the others). They may be three alternative scenarios for how you may want to live your life—or they may be building blocks to reach something you want. Once you have labeled this pathway, describe what you need to do each year over the time period you have selected. These are things you will need to do, accomplish, or resolve for this pathway to create the life you want.

Describe them in the spaces below.

Description of Pathway #1:

What will you do this year?

What will you do in year 2?

What will you do in year 3?

What will you do in year 4?

What will you do in year 5?

Description of Pathway #2:

What will you do this year?

What will you do in year 2?

What will you do in year 3?

What will you do in year 4?

What will you do in year 5?

Description of Pathway #3:

What will you do this year?

What will you do in year 2?

What will you do in year 3?

What will you do in year 4?

What will you do in year 5?

This has been important planning work. You are narrowing and focusing the things you want to do and be during this next stage of your life. When you are ready, you can take this planning to a more defined plan of action. To do this, select one of these areas for further development. Answer the questions that are outlined on the worksheet below. You may want to do this for all three areas if that would be helpful, but for now, address only one area (or a combination if appropriate).

- Give this pathway or priority a name and write a brief summary of what you want to accomplish, develop, or create.
- What resources will you need to make this successful? This may include financial resources, skills, knowledge, or assistance from other people. Identify what is needed or what needs to be determined.
- How will you monitor and reinforce your actions? What are the critical milestones that will tell you how well you are progressing with getting what you want? How can you keep yourself engaged and motivated?
- What obstacles may you encounter? What difficulties may you face? What do you think you can do about them? How confident are you that you will be able to do what you've said (low, medium, or high)?
- How well are these tasks aligned with what you know about yourself and your unique abilities? What are the attributes, abilities, or talents you have that will build on or utilize for these tasks?
- What difference will it make? If you are successful, what impact will this likely have on you or others? Why is doing these actions important to you?
- How will you begin? There is an old saying that a thousand-mile journey begins with a single step. This is the time for you to determine those first few steps for getting started.

Now, let's develop your Master Plan.

Your Primary Pathway: The name for this is thing you want to do?

1. Summarize what you want to accomplish, develop, create or do:

2. What resources will you need to do this? (People, money, legal, facilities, equipment, etc.)

3. Identify 2 or 3 milestones to track and reinforce your progress. Note what and when.

4. What obstacles might you likely encounter? How will you address them?

5. Which unique abilities, skills or talents will you utilize?

6. What difference will this make to you or others? Why is this important to you?

7. How will you begin? What are your immediate next steps?

Final Step to Your Master Plan: Write Yourself a Letter

As the final step to your Master Plan, write yourself a letter. In this letter, express what action you will take and why these actions are important to you. Also, describe any primary concerns you have about this. What would happen if nothing were done? What would happen if you were very successful?

When you have completed this letter to yourself, sign and date it. It is important to make this commitment to yourself so that this plan is more than just words on a page. This letter, this Master Plan, is what is important to you to move into the next stage, see the opportunities, and realize the importance of this time for you in the next stage of reinventing your adulthood.

Dear _____:

Sincerely,

Date:

Chapter 10
Holding On and Letting Go

*Between stimulus and response there is a space in our power to choose
our response. In our response lies our growth and our freedom.*
—Victor Frankl, *Man's Search for Meaning*

Throughout the book, I have provided information, references, ideas, and tools to guide you through your unique and special discovery process. We began by looking at the context of a lifetime in stages. You are not at the end of life, but you are closer to the end than to the beginning. This has important implications for what you do during this time period. This is indeed a new time in the history of human civilization, and we are developing precedents for generations that follow. So, in this chapter, we will reflect and understand the process of change on which you are about to embark on—or are currently working through. There will be things that you want to hold on to because they provide important meaning to you at this time, and there will be things you will want to let go of because they are no longer important or necessary for you. The key goal is to enable you, when that time comes, to look back on your life and know it was well lived. Let the journey you've taken speak for who you are.

It is no wonder that there is a lot being written and promoted about this time of life. There are major commercial opportunities, and companies and entrepreneurs understand the wants that are there, the numbers of people, and the financial resources that they have. It is no wonder that industries are being reshaped and recalibrated to take advantage of opportunities created by people entering this stage. Other industries are fearing this transformation in our society. Like how the baby boom generation reshaped school systems and American politics in the sixties and seventies, they are again reshaping how society responds to new demands and challenges to the conventional order of retirement.

This is indeed a time of transition. David saw the process initially as gradual as he started gaining greater control over his time. Each step took him from familiar territory to the unknown, less defined or structured, and more personal. "I initially felt guilty for having time when my friends were heading off to work. But when I went for jury duty and they asked me if I was employed or retired, the answer got stuck in my throat." He realized he was entering the next stage and didn't know what he was going to do or how he was going to describe who he was.

Understanding the Transitions

There are several descriptions of the transition process as one goes into this Reinventing adulthood stage of life. In *Creative Aging*, Marjory Zoet Bankson describes the process of change that one experiences as one progresses into this next stage.[99] There is initially a great *release* as you leave the workplace, and you experience the most dramatic shift in what has been your life activities. If you are doing it in stages, there comes a point when you feel the balance has shifted. Something is fundamentally different. Then, a feeling of *resistance* emerges, and you start to feel the dramatic nature of change and the implications it has on existing relationships, income, and identity. This time may be accompanied by feelings of anger, disappointment, and a desire to quickly get back into something to fill the void.

Over time, you start to understand the importance of this time. You become more possessive of your time, and you work to *reclaim* this time. You can move forward onto new things that are better suited to what you want to become or pursue. At some point, there is a *revelation* when you discover the wonders of the stage and the openness it provides. You

---

[99]   Bankson, Marjory Zoet, *Creative Aging: Rethinking Retirement and Non-Retirement in a Changing World*, Skylight Paths Publishing, Woodstock, VT, 2010.

may discover or rediscover your sense of purpose and mission. There is new insight and excitement.

There is another point when you cross over from ideas and inspiration to *restructure* your life differently. You start aligning the things you are doing with the feelings and wants you have for this time. You sense that you are beginning again. You are setting up new structures in your life that are important. Along with this comes a sense of *risk-taking* because you don't know if what you are doing will provide the fulfillment you seek. You likely feel nervous and excited about what is now new. Fear and excitement are feelings that are closely related. You have a sense that you are moving up a spiral and not working around a circle. The change process concludes with a sense of *reinvention*, where you have reached a new place in your life. Here, you are finding your way, you are experiencing what you envisioned, and it is becoming your new reality. You may change what you are doing, stop some things, and start new ones because you can. Each time you progress to what appears like you are back at the beginning, you realize that you are progressing upward. You continue to learn, gain wisdom, expand your perspectives, and feel all right.

When you transition from your employer to this new stage, it may often be necessary and important to take time to detox or let the pressures, habits, wants, and resentments fade away. There is little you can do about them now, and it is often better to let them go than to hold on to them with the hope that someday you'll be able to resolve them. Today is the day to let them go.

Further, it is important to not rush into something too fast. Many have found that when they did, they ended up making mistakes and creating greater issues for themselves. Be thoughtful and curious. Experiment with different things until you find the right set of activities. You may also realize that even the things that are important to you now may evolve and become less important and less crucial to your happiness over time. You're not making a career or life commitment at this time; you retain the ability and responsibility to keep yourself flexible and free. Use the insights of your Master Plan to guide you forward.

We can see these changes by viewing what others have experienced as they entered and progressed in this time for reinvention. When Peter

C. left his employer, he tried a new company for a while. He found that the relationships were not the same, the work was similar but less inspiring, and the crises were less engaging. He soon realized that he jumped too soon into an employment situation and that there was something else he wanted to do. He quit without another place to go. This was an important step for him to take.

Peter soon realized that he loved cooking. He took a class in cooking—and then another and then another. He was watching his post-career career evolve into being a chef. It was the perfect mix of doing something part-time (and retaining the time flexibility he wanted), being with other people with whom he shared a common passion and feeling the intensity of an engagement that can often only be found in the kitchen of a major restaurant. Although the money is a lot less than what he earned in his career, he is as engaged and entertained as he wants to be. He has other things he wants to do as well and has the time and energy to pursue them.

Toby discovered that she was empowered to make her own decisions about how to invest her time and talents. She no longer needed to do things because other people expected her to do them. She had choices. She didn't expect to be feeling this when she was transitioning from a successful career in communication. "It is sometimes hard to appreciate yourself when you've put the interests of others ahead of yourself for many years. But now the tables have turned, and this is not being inconsiderate of others—I'm just being able to be me."

When Dean retired after many years of working for a technology company, he knew he had many interests. As we learned earlier, he entered this time of retirement with some degree of positive anticipation. This time affords him opportunities to explore new things and reclaim some old interests. He is using the transition time to go deeper into some areas of current passion and then see what he ultimately wants to do for the long-term. He worries that he lacks a sense of direction and purpose, and he wonders if this is something he should work on. He sometime worries about whether he is productive—but then he realizes that doing what he really wants to do is being productive. This is an important realization for him.

Reflecting on the Meaning of This Stage

This Reinventing stage is not a monolithic experience, where you work through your transition and then you are set until you find yourself in the Consolidation stage. It is not ten, twenty, or thirty years of doing the same thing. It evolves and transforms based on interests, opportunities, and fate. Illnesses may come suddenly and be more intense, or the loss of a spouse may change everything. Things that used to make you excited and interested may fade and lose some of their appeal. New things and ideas emerge that may captivate your interests for a time.

One of the interviewees described this time was like when you were a freshman in college, but all the world is your campus now. If you are sixty now, and your Consolidation stage doesn't come until you are ninety, then you have thirty years in front of you. If you have less time, well, you just have less time. It is very important for you to begin now. You have the freedom to pursue your current priorities and let them evolve and change—and change you.

The process of defining how you will spend this stage of life will be dependent on many things. First, we examined how you will or should spend your time. This is the last time in your life when you will be able to pursue the things that are most meaningful to you. You will have the physical and mental abilities to do something different or do something deeper. You have probably passed your child-rearing age and perhaps ended your formal career. You have accomplished what you wanted—or tried to—and your striving for that promotion, next job, or special award is now in the past. It is your time, and you can decide how you want to use it. At the core of this opportunity are the things that energize and engage you. They utilize your strengths, hidden and known, and clarify your wants. You will know and feel your responsibilities.

Research is showing that the value you receive from engaging in a particular action, activity, or mission comes from the feelings it generates in you. Your assignment is to experience what is most meaningful to you through your "feelings filter." So, your challenge is to determine what you want (the feelings and experiences you want to have) and how to realize them in the most effective way you can. This may sound like an overly logical process, but it is a lot more than logic. It means that you need to dig deep inside of yourself to find the calling that defines who you are and what you want to be and then find the best path to take you there. Remember that happiness often comes from pursuing meaning.

While you are defining your personal mission, you also have the challenge to live responsibly. In short, this means living within your means so that money does not become a crisis in your life. Some people do not need to worry about whether they will have sufficient financial resources to pursue whatever journey they want. Most people will face challenges. The challenge to those who need to pay attention to their financial resources is to be creative, resourceful, and thoughtful about what they do. It is a time to define your wants within the context of your means, and most importantly, create experiences that you enjoy. Envy of those with money is a feeling that will distract you from your calling and your compass. Feelings of depression, wanting more, or being limited are normal given the conditions you face, but they don't need to define who you are or what you do. This is a time to open yourself to alternatives and create directions that will provide the feelings you want to experience in a manner that is responsible. Consider the word *responsible* as the conjunction between two concepts: *response* and *able*. It is how you respond that will make the difference to your experiences in this next stage of your life.

The next area we explored in this book is how your relationships will change based on the changes you make during this stage of your life. This includes both your primary relationships as well as the series of concentric circles of family and friends that compose your world. For some people who are leaving a strong work place culture, with lots of important relationships, the separation will be difficult. You are likely to feel both release and grief from losing these connections. Social media provides opportunities to stay connected to these old friends, but the relationships will not be the same. Informal, spontaneous encounters often fulfill our needs for affiliation and affection. This loss cannot be underestimated in terms of the gap created by this change. This will be a time to identify who you want to hold on to—and who you want to let go of—and rebuild your community.

We are creatures who are highly dependent on relationships. They are often the only thing we have as we progress through the next stages of life. Relationships are the source that keeps us grounded. They bring us up when we're down and provide a bridge when times are tough. The task we have is to understand what we need and want, to identify who is the best fit for what, and to nurture these relationships.

Benjamin Franklin once said, "If you want to be loved, then love and be loveable."

Eleanor Roosevelt said, "Since you get more joy out of giving joy to others, you should put a good deal of thought into the happiness that you are able to give."

Relationships are what you create.

Health is like an "infrastructure factor" in life. Without it, other things will be difficult. But this is not a binary condition. You are neither healthy nor not healthy. You live on a continuum of health that influences your ability to pursue what you want. We all have some physical challenges; some have many more than others. These conditions often define what we can and cannot do to some degree. However, it does not take away from the feelings that can be experienced.

What is also quite interesting is that our health is highly dependent on our own past and present behaviors. If you have not taken care of yourself in the past, then today is a good day to start. Research has shown that people who start exercising regularly—at least three times per week—often live longer and live better even if they don't start until their midsixties.[100] It is harder if you wait till you're in your midseventies or beyond, but it is better to start anytime than to give up. We explored ways to retain your health through diets that are based primarily on fruits, vegetables, and whole grains, regular exercise, and actions that are personal ways you can take care of yourself. We all know what is right to do; the challenge is that we seldom do what we should do. There are clearly things in our current lifestyles that reinforce actions that don't benefit us. The immediacy of satisfaction often outweighs the value of long-term conditioning. Therefore, the challenge is to make healthy living habits fun and satisfying in ways that are greater than current sedentary or harmful practices.

---

[100] Harvard Medical School Special Health Report, "Living Better, Living Longer," Harvard Health Publications, 2017.

If you carefully examine your current healthy living habits, you may find that you do some things well, and some things you do or don't do actually can create harm. Unfortunately, the real harm may be in the future and not felt by you today, but by understanding the impact of the extra calories, the sedentary lifestyle, and excessive consumption of certain things, you will become dissatisfied with the status quo. Without this sense of dissatisfaction, there is likely to be little change or little urgency to change. Start there and see what you are doing to yourself that may in fact shorten or inhibit your ability to live the life you imagine. Examine closely the things that you are doing or not doing that may bring harm to you in the future. Understand why you continue to pursue them today and determine whether today's satisfaction is worth the pain or problem this may create for yourself in the future. We know from behavior science that positive reinforcements that are certain and short term have more influence on our behaviors than positive reinforcements that are uncertain or in the future. So, what can you do now to change and start doing those things that will provide you with greater value in the future? Can you do a little bit of this change today? Think about how this will make you feel—today and in the future.

Take a moment and reread the quote from Victor Frankl at the beginning of this chapter. He gained this insight from his experience as a Holocaust survivor and seeing the difference between those who survived and those who gave up. At the core, at those moments when we can feel this or feel that, we make a choice. We have the power of choice, and that is an important lesson to remember.

Finally, the vision you have for yourself needs to integrate all the key elements we've covered to this point. It can provide you with options, alternatives, and adventures. It can enable you to find and do those elements of life that create the greatest meaning and enable you—perhaps for the first time in your life—to pursue those things that are of great interest to you. You may think of this as a "portfolio of life activities" or "micro-stages" of different styles of living. Ultimately, you will find a balance that you will discover with pride, importance, and perhaps a little humor.

Both Dick and Richard (referred to earlier) have moved past their income-generating work activities. Dick is no longer practicing medicine even a few days per month. He continues to do his blogs on integrating exercise and other healthy habits with other fun things. Richard has stopped being an adjunct professor because it was just too little money for the amount of effort. While he misses his students, he is expanding some of his other areas of interest. He is making more furniture and is more engaged in his music. He is doing longer exciting travels. He is enjoying this time immensely. They have both passed through an initial stage of retirement life and found even more engaging activities. They have both found ways to live responsibly, integrate a lot of exercise into their daily routines and adventure vacations, and retain a strong community of friends. Stephanie has finished many of her travel adventures and has returned to doing some consulting and coaching, some for pay and some for free. She feels her life has become enriched by this stage, and she is planning her next lifestyle adventure.

Betsy says, "I am responsible for my own happiness. I like the work I do and the relationships I've had over many years. I work to keep my life in balance. While I'm not always successful at keeping this balance, I do those things that I am good at—and it makes a difference in the lives of others." She says she will know when it is time to move on, but for now, she stays engaged.

Creating the Life You Want

Take some time now to review what you said was important about your time, financial conditions, relationships, identity, and lifestyle. Imagine yourself as driven by an inner purpose, secure in your situation, with those you love and who love you, and healthy, fit, flexible, and resilient. How does this make you feel? What about the possibility of being that person? Can you do that? Can you be that?

As you realize the challenges you must now face, appreciate what you have. You just need to get started. Don't create a New Year's resolution or promises you won't keep. This is not for someone else; this is for you. Identify small steps that start moving you forward and give you a strong sense of satisfaction, joy, and pleasure. Do things that are fun *and* healthy for you. Celebrate and appreciate those steps—even the small ones at first. Start small and then build on what you have learned and accomplished.

The changes that you are embarking on will bring something to you that you never had before. They will bring back the things that you perhaps once lost or always wanted. This is a time to look forward and backward, hold on to what is important, and let go of things you no longer need. This is your time; your chapter is now ready to be written.

This is the time when you will be redefining your identity and selecting the brand, image, or persona you want to be known for. You can try something on for a while and see how it goes. Of course, at the beginning, you will feel uncomfortable and incompetent. You may have a deliberate mission and go after it. You may find that it was not that important after all, you were not able to realize what you sought, or you gradually lost interest in whatever captured your imagination earlier.

As you let go and move away from things that used to define you and provide a great sense of satisfaction, new things will emerge. Is there a force within you that you are discovering? Is this really what or how you want to be? Does this align with other things around you? Have you experienced seemingly random acts that somehow encourage your new direction? Perhaps you found a hidden treasure that has unlocked something important. This is the time in life when discovery is really possible. You no longer are burdened by external responsibilities, a workplace, a family, your children, or other obligations. Listen to that voice and seek to understand what it is saying to you. Stay focused on finding and discovering who you are really intended to become.

I grew up in Oklahoma. When I was a child, my godmother would take me to Native American powwows because she was one-quarter Cherokee Indian. She wanted me to experience and appreciate this culture in our society.

When I was in my early teens and attended one of the powwows, I passed an old man sitting outside a teepee. It was late afternoon, and the air hung cool. As I passed, he said, "Son, do you know how to ride a horse across a raging river?"

I stopped. My father had taught me to always be polite. I said, "No, sir. I don't." I knew that I was about to hear something interesting, profound, or just weird. I was a young teenager who was looking forward to driving a car, discovering girls, and playing with my friends, but I paused at this point to listen.

The old gentlemen beckoned me to sit down.

I did. I was polite and respectful.

He said, "The way you ride a horse across a raging river is to focus your attention on a point on the horizon. It could be a tree, a mountain, a cloud, or something far in front of you. Then, as you gradually enter the river, be one with the horse, and together pull yourself through the waters. Keep yourself focused on that point on the horizon. Let the horse take you there. If you stop, freeze up, try to take control, and look down, you will surely swamp. Keep your eyes and mind focused on that point on the horizon."

I said thank you, shook his hand, and moved on. He wanted nothing in return, but somehow, I was changed.

I learned the importance of focusing on something greater than myself. I learned to appreciate the trust and connection of my companions. I learned to keep moving forward, being somehow magically pulled toward what I was meant to do, whatever it will be.

One of the phrases I used frequently throughout this book is one that I want to feel when it is my time to move on to what is after this life. I want to be able to look back and say with honesty, "This was a life well lived." I want to know that I have made the best of what I have been given—both opportunities and challenges. I want to live this next stage with a sense of hope and not regret. I want to experience meaning, engagement, and fulfillment. I want to know that somehow, I've made the world a better place, even if only in small ways.

So, I leave you with these thoughts and perspectives. Now is the time to make the changes you want and continue doing the things that are important to you. Time is not on your side. If not now, when? This is the time for you to discover what is engaging and meaningful. Now is the time to create the life you want—and you have the ultimate responsibility to make it so. Look forward to the time when you can honestly say that the life you've led speaks for you—and that this life was well lived.

"Let the Life I Lead"
Julee Glaub Weems and Mark Weems

Let the life I lead, speak for me.
Let the life I lead, speak for me.
When I'm lying in my grave
And there's nothing more to say,
Let the life I lead speak for me.

Let the friends I've had, speak for me.
Let the friends I've had, speak for me.
When I'm lying in my grave
And there's nothing more to say,
Let the friends I've had speak for me.

Let the love I've shared, speak for me.
Let the love I've shared, speak for me.
When I'm lying in my grave
And there's nothing more to say,
Let the love I've shared speak for me.

Let the work I did, speak for me.
Let the work I did, speak for me.
When I'm lying in my grave,
And there's nothing more to say,
Let the work I did, speak for me.

Let the songs I sang, speak for me.
Let the songs I sang, speak for me.
When I'm lying in my grave
And there's nothing more to say.
Let the songs I sang, speak for me.

Let the life I lead, speak for me.
Let the life I lead, speak for me.
When I'm lying in my grave,
And there's nothing more to say,
Let the life I lead, speak for me.

*The song can be found on "Healing at the Roots"
www.littlewindows.net
Permission granted, Julee Glaub Weems and Mark Weems

Bibliography

Arrien, Angeles, *The Second Half of Life: Opening the Eight Gates of Wisdom*, Boulder, CO, Sounds True, 2007.

Baltes, P. B. (1987). "Theoretical propositions of life-span developmental psychology: On the dynamics between growth and decline," *Developmental Psychology*, 23(5), 611–626.

Baltes, P. B., Lindenberger, U., & Staudinger, U. M. (2006). "Life span theory in developmental psychology." In R. M. Lerner & W. Damon (Eds.), Handbook *of Child Psychology: Theoretical Models of Human Development* (569–664). Hoboken, NJ: John Wiley.

Bankson, Marjory Zoet, *Creative Aging*, SkyLight Paths Publishers, Woodstock, VT, 2010.

Bateson, Mary Catherine, *Composing a Further Life: The Age of Active Wisdom*, Vintage Books, New York, NY, 2010.

Bjorklund, B.R. *The Journey of Adulthood*. Prentice Hall.

Bowling, A., & Dieppe, P. "What is successful aging and who should define it?" *British Medical Journal*, 331(7531), 1548–1551. doi:10.1136/bmj.331.7531.1548, 2005.

Bridges, William, *Transitions: Making Sense of Life's Changes*, Cambridge, MA, Da Capo Press, 2004.

Broderick, P., Blewitt, C., *The Life Span: Human Development for Helping Professionals*, Pearson Publishing, 2014, 4th edition.

Buettner, Dan, *The Blue Zones: Nine Lessons for Living Longer*, National Geographic, Washington, DC, 2008.

Burnett, Bill and Dave Evans, *Designing Your Life: How to Build a Well-lived Joyful Life*, Knopf Publishers, New York, 2016.

Casey, Tom and Karen Warlin, *Executive Transitions: A Guide for Transitioning Executives and the Companies that Employ Them*, Telemachus Press, LLC, www.discussonpartners.com, 2013.

Cavanaugh, J. C., & Blanchard-Fields, F. "Where people live: Person-environment interactions." *Adult Development and Aging* (7th ed., 127–156). Stamford, CT: Cengage Learning, 2015.

Chittister, Joan, *The Gift of Years: Growing Older Gracefully*, New York, BlueBridge, 2008.

Corbett, David, *Portfolio Life: The New Path to Work Purpose and Passion After 50*, John Wiley & Sons Publishers, San Francisco, CA, 2007.

Dainese, S. M., Allemand, M., Ribeiro, N., Bayram, S., Martin, M., & Ehlert, U. "Protective factors in midlife: How do people stay healthy?" *The Journal of Gerontopsychology and Geriatric Psychiatry*, 24(1), 19, 2011.

Donnellan, M. B., & Lucas, R. E. "Age differences in the Big Five across the life span: evidence from two national samples." *Psychology and Aging*, 23(3), 558, 2008.

Erikson, E. H., *Identity and the Life Cycle*. London: W. W. Norton & Co., 1980.

Frankl, Victor E., *Man's Search for Meaning*, Beacon Press, Boston, MA, 2006.

Gratton, Lynda and Andrew Scott, *The 100-Year Life: Living and Working in an Age of Longevity*, Bloomsbury Business Publications, New York, 2017.

Hagerty, Barbara Bradley, *Life Reimagined: The Science, Art, and Opportunity of Midlife*, Riverbend Books, New York, 2016.

Hansson, R. O., & Stroebe, M. S. "Bereavement in late life: Coping, adaptation, and developmental influences," *American Psychological Association*, 2007.

Hayflick, L. "How and why we age," *Experimental Gerontology*, 33, 639–653, 1998.

Hermann, M., Untergasser, G., Rumpold, H., and Berger, P. "Aging of the male reproductive system," *Experimental Gerontology*, 35(9–10), 1267–1279, 2000.

Hollis, James, *Finding Meaning in the Second Half of Life: How to Finally Really Grow Up*, New York, Gotham Books, 2005.

Hurme, Sally Balch, *Get the Most Out of Retirement*, published by AARP, 2017.

Jason, Julie, *The AARP Retirement Survival Guide by the American Association of Retired Persons*, Sterling Publishing, 2009.

Jung, Carl C., Memories, *Dreams and Reflections*, Vintage Books, New York, 1965.

Kahana, E., Kelley-Moore, J., & Kahana, B. "Proactive aging: A longitudinal study of stress, resources, agency, and well-being in late life," *Aging & Mental Health*, 16(4), 438–451, 2012.

Kim, J. E., & Moen, P. (2001). "Is retirement good or bad for subjective well-being?" *Current Directions in Psychological Science*, 10(3), 83–86. doi: 10.1111/1467-8721.00121.

Harvard's Brain-Mind Science Center website: www.brain.harvard.edu/center-brain-science.

Lawrence-Lightfoot, Sara, *The Third Chapter: Passion, Risk, and Adventure in the 25 years after 50*, New York, Farrar, Straus & Giroux, 2009.

Leider, R. J. *The Power of Purpose: Finding Meaning, Live Longer, Better.* Berrett-Koehler Publishers, 3rd edition, 2015.

Levinson, D.J. "A conception of adult development," *American Psychologist*, 41, 3–13, 1986.

Levinson, D. J., *The Seasons of a Man's Life*, Alfred A. Knopf, New York. 1986.

Leon, G. R., Gillum, B., Gillum, R., & Gouze, M., "Personality stability and change over a 30-year period—middle age to old age," *Journal of Consulting and Clinical Psychology*, 47(3), 517.

"Living Better, Living Longer," Special Report from the Harvard Medical School, Robert Schneiber, MD, Medical Editor, Anne Underwood Executive Editor, Bolvoir Medical Group, Norwalk, CT, 2017.

Quinn, Jane Bryant, *How to Make Your Money Last: The Indispensable Retirement Guide*, Simon and Schuster Publishers, 2016.

Rogers, C., *On Becoming a Person*, Houghton Mifflin, New York, 1996.

Rowe, J., & Kahn, R. "Successful aging," *The Gerontologist*, 37(4), 433–440. doi:10.1093/geront/37.4.433, 1997.

Ryan, Robin, *Retirement Reinvention: Make Your Next Act Your Best Act*, Penguin Books, 2018.

Schaie, K. W. *Adult Development and Aging.* Pearson Publishing Co., 2001.

Scherer, John J., *Five Questions That Change Everything: Life Lessons at Work*, Fort Collins, CO, Word Keepers, 2009.

Seeman, T. E., Lusignolo, T. M., Albert, M., & Berkman, L., "Social relationships, social support, and patterns of cognitive aging in healthy, high-functioning older adults: MacArthur studies of successful aging," *Health Psychology*, 20(4), 243–255. doi: 10.1037/0278-6133.20.4.243, 2001.

Shulman, N. "Life-cycle variations in patterns of close relationships," *Journal of Marriage and Family*, 37 (4, Special Section: Macrosociology of the Family), 813–821, 1975.

Smith, Hyrum W., *Purposeful Retirement: How to Bring Happiness and Meaning to Your Retirement*, Mango Publications, Coral Gables, FL, 2017.

Srivastava, S., John, O. P., Gosling, S. D., & Potter, J., "Development of personality in early and middle adulthood: Set like plaster or persistent change?" *Journal of Personality and Social Psychology*, 84(5), 1041–1053. doi:10.1037/0022-3514.84.5.1041, 2003.

Urry, H. L., & Gross, J. J., "Emotion regulation in older age," *Current Directions in Psychological Science*, 19(6), 352–357, 2010.

Wrzus, C., Hänel, M., Wagner, J., & Neyer, F. J., "Social network changes and life events across the life span: A meta-analysis," *Psychological Bulletin*, 139(1), 53-80. doi: 10.1037/a0028601, 2013.

Zelinski, Ernie, *How to Retire Happy, Wild & Free: Retirement Wisdom That You Won't Get from Your Financial Advisor*, Visions International Publishing, 2009.

About the Author

As a nationally recognized author and management consultant, Tom Wilson is a master problem-solver, synthesizer and communicator. His career has focused on taking complex information and making it simple to understand and to act upon. As he began entering his "Next Stage," he decided to see what it was like and how to make it purposeful and fulfilling.

Tom is the author of three books and over 30 articles and book chapters. He has a Master's Degree in business and enjoys conducting special research on trends, best practices and new discoveries. He has used these skills to create a book that helps the reader understand and focus one's life in new directions as they enter their retirement years.

Tom has presented his works to groups throughout the world. He enjoys engaging with his audience, presenting new perspectives to complex challenges, and sharing interesting stories. If you would like Tom to present and engage your group, contact him at the address below:

Tom@MyNextStage.org
www.MyNextStage.org

CPSIA information can be obtained
at www.ICGtesting.com
Printed in the USA
FSHW011029060919
61739FS